JUST TELL THEM

THE POWER OF
EXPLANATIONS
AND EXPLICIT
TEACHING

ZACH GROSHELL, PhD

FROM HODDER EDUCATION

To order, please visit www.johncatt.com or contact Customer Service at education@hachette.co.uk / +44 (0)1235 827827.

ISBN: 978 1 0360 0368 5

© Zach Groshell 2024

First published in 2024 by
John Catt from Hodder Education,
An Hachette UK Company
15 Riduna Park, Station Road,
Melton, Woodbridge IP12 1QT
www.johncatt.com

Cover artwork © Shutterstock/Jozef Micic

Photo credits: Figure 5a © Shutterstock/Bilanol, Figure 5b © Shutterstock/ Antonio Solano, Figures 5c and 5d © Shutterstock/Davco Media, teacher cartoons © Shutterstock/Lemono

Typeset in the UK.

Printed in the UK.

A catalogue record for this title is available from the British Library.

To Stephanie, June, and Rose

CONTENTS

FOREWORD

EXPLAINING EXPLAINED

Humans are (almost) unique among animal sorts in that they are capable of communicating what they have learnt to others who haven't yet learnt it. We've done that through oral histories, pictographs, written histories, and just plain teaching. This information communication from adults to adults, children to children, parents to children, teachers to students, and so forth are all ways in which humans convey what they know to other humans. Another word for this is teaching. Our cognitive architecture has evolved and is set up to do this and is based upon the first two of the five natural information processing system principles as proposed by John and Susan Sweller .

The first principle – the information store principle – suggests that, in order to function, natural information processing systems require an enormous store of information. This is what our long-term memory does with respect to human cognition. All of what each of us has learnt is stored in our long-term memory and is accessible to us when we need it. The second principle – the borrowing and reorganizing principle – implies that most of the information acquired by and stored in long-term memory is borrowed from the long-term memories of other people. We listen to what they say, read what they write, have it explained to us (we 'borrow' that information from those sources). Once that information is acquired from others, we reorganize it by using information that we have previously acquired and stored in our long-term memory as knowledge.

Explaining, as defined and discussed in this book, makes use of these two principles. This explaining 'lends' the information of one person (a teacher, the authors of textbooks, other experts) to others (their students, listeners, readers). The teacher then helps them, through the specific instructional techniques discussed in the book, to reorganize that 'borrowed' information in their own long-term memories; that is, in the already existing knowledge schemas in their long-term memory. You could say, explaining is the epitome of what makes us human. And to either neglect or even deny this, denies our uniqueness as species and hampers our teaching and learning.

Paul A. Kirschner
Emeritus Professor of Educational Psychology at the
Open University of the Netherlands

ABOUT THE AUTHOR

Zach Groshell, PhD is a highly distinguished teacher, instructional coach, and education consultant. Zach is based in the Seattle area and works with schools around the globe to develop high-quality instruction based on the science of how students learn. Zach hosts the podcast Progressively Incorrect and is active on X @mrzachg and on his blog, educationrickshaw.com.

INTRODUCTION

When I was training to be a teacher, my professors were fond of explaining to us how much more there is to teaching than explaining.

He who does the talking, does the learning (they explained to us from behind their podiums).

Your job is to be a guide on the side, not a sage on the stage (they explained to us from a literal stage).

And then there was the mother of all edu-babble; that virtue-signaling, cringe-inducing, absolute nothingburger of a statement that still makes its rounds on social media and education conferences.

I don't teach students. They teach me.

It was rather ironic that my professors used teacher talk to diminish the importance of teacher talk. But at the time, their words had an impact on me. I, too, held contempt for the boring, long-winded, unrelenting lectures that I was forced to endure as a student.

If teachers talked less, the students would take more ownership over their learning, I thought.

When I would analyze the flatlining achievement of American students – a problem that persists to this day (NAEP, 2023) – I became convinced that the source of our problem was education's reliance on the traditional, teacher-led model of instruction. "Traditional" conjured black-and-white images of passive children, forced to regurgitate facts in bolted-down desks, driven by a stern, ruler-wielding disciplinarian.

If teacher talk worked, we wouldn't be in this mess, I concluded.

Wanting to do right by my students, I spent an enormous amount of effort at the start of my teaching career trying to heed the advice of my professors and the disciples they'd trained. I'd start a lesson by, for example, putting poster paper on the floor and passing out markers in order to "investigate" what the students were thinking. I'd design large, open ended tasks and projects, and have students sitting in all sorts of creative arrangements, facing away from me and towards each other. Cardboard and yarn spilled out of my classroom's doorway, and I took pride in all the movement and noise my students were making.

I especially took pride in my ability to *resist* explaining the material to students. When a student needed help, I would ask lots of probing questions to try to get them to arrive at the solution on their own. Sometimes I would place my finger on a key element of their work, my lips sealed in a cheeky smile, and exit the scene to allow space for the student to get themselves unstuck. Whenever a student directly asked me to explain the material to them, I would encourage them to use their thinking skills, or consult a friend or the internet. In the hierarchy of teaching options, I considered explanation to be the tool of last resort.

If I tell them, I narrated to myself, *I will only take away their opportunity to discover it on their own.*

If these descriptions of my first years of teaching appeal to you, I'm sorry to say you may not like the rest of this book. After years of experimenting on students with these groovy methods, I eventually had to come to grips with the fact that it wasn't working out so well. Every time I tried to get my students to discover stuff, the only students who benefited were those who already knew a lot about the material. Everyone else would be visibly relieved whenever I paused their meandering explorations to demystify the material through clear and concise explanations.

I came to realize that effective teaching is not about keeping information from kids, but about providing the information kids need to think about and getting them to think hard about it. To do this, I would need to reclaim my role as the primary source of information and replace much of the unstructured discovery time that I'd failed to make work with expertly crafted explanations.

OVERVIEW

This book is all about showing, telling, demonstrating, modeling, presenting, and yes, explaining. In contrast to the book's cheeky title, it places a substantial emphasis on how explanations are integrated into an explicit teaching system. By paying special attention to the cognitive science underpinnings of effective explanation, and the insights from teacher effectiveness research and Direct Instruction (DI), my goal is to equip you with the tools you need to convey ideas with impact and clarity.

The first chapter delves into the "why" behind explanation, introducing the cognitive architecture and worked example effect, then each chapter will focus on an area of explanation. These are:

- Explain with undivided attention: Set the conditions for focus
- Explain clearly: Say only the words that need to be said
- Explain interactively: Alternate between inputs and outputs
- Explain with visuals: Pair speaking with images and drawings
- Explain with examples: Show what it is and what it isn't
- Explain with stories: Use narrative, emotion, and gestures
- Explain and release: Gradually fade guidance
- Conclusion.

Let's begin, shall we?

WHY EXPLAIN?

Explanations, when delivered with precision, are highly effective for learning. This becomes evident when we recognize that the mind is finely tuned to acquire information from others (Paas & van Merriënboer, 2020). However, students are not like sponges, effortlessly absorbing all the information we wish them to learn. Each student possesses a "cognitive architecture" with inherent limitations and constraints that must be understood for effective learning to occur.

To grasp why, when, and how explaining is so impactful, we need to delve into this "cognitive architecture." We're not going to talk about pre-frontal cortexes and myelination and hippocampi and other neuro-speak. We're going to talk mainly about two structures: working memory and long-term memory.

WORKING MEMORY

All students are endowed with a **working memory**, the structure that handles conscious thinking and information processing. Anything that is "outside" of the learner, from the teacher's spoken words to the images on their PowerPoint slides, must be grappled with in working memory if it is to be learned. Right now, as you read these words, you are "working" with those words in the site called working memory (see Figure 1).

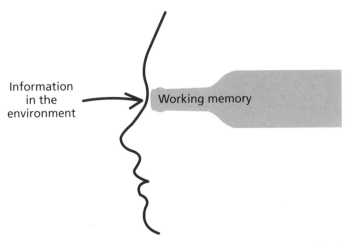

Figure 1: Information outside the learner must be processed (i.e. thought about) in working memory if it is to be learned

The problem is, all working memories are easily overwhelmed. Students can only hold a small number of items in working memory at a time, and for only a few seconds, before that information starts to slip away (Cowan, 2001; Miller, 1956). Because working memory is so small and limited, we often refer to it as the "bottleneck" of learning (see Figure 1). The information we want students to learn must first pass through narrow working memory, but if we're not careful about how we design and deliver the information we put in it, the **cognitive load** they experience will be too heavy, and learning won't take place.

As an example of having your working memory "overloaded," imagine that you are required to hold all your friends' food orders in mind just long enough to complete an order over the phone. Most of us are perfectly capable of handling two or three simple orders at a time, but will struggle to remember any more unless we write them down. With each increase in the number or complexity of the orders (or if we're bombarded with distractions or last-minute changes), our ability to complete the task decreases further. Our limited working memories can only handle so much.

Instruction is often designed without consideration for working memory limitations. Sometimes, as was the case with the loosie-goosie "discovery approach" I used at the start of my career, cognitive overload is caused by withholding the explanations that students need to make sense of what they're doing. We will return to this idea shortly, after we take a look at long-term memory, the storehouse for all the knowledge and skills we learn.

LONG-TERM MEMORY

The other structure of the human cognitive architecture that we must attend to as teachers is **long-term memory**. While thought breaks down when the limitations of working memory are exceeded, there is no known limit to the capacity of long-term memory (see Figure 2).

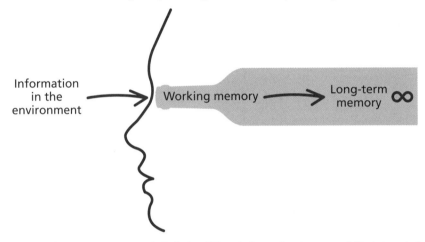

Figure 2: Long-term memory is infinite. When information is successfully integrated into long-term memory, learning has taken place

As Figure 2 shows, information outside the learner must first pass through an extremely limited working memory to be embedded in long-term memory, where it links up with everything the learner already knows: their facts, skills, and past experiences. When information becomes internalized in long-term memory, the information has been learned. Consequently, we now have a **definition of learning**: Learning is a change in long-term memory.

The most powerful characteristic of long-term memory is how it interacts with working memory to enable students to think critically and creatively, and to solve problems in their environment. While working memory is like the "gatekeeper" to long-term memory, and thus requires us to carefully manage the cognitive load of tasks so as not to overwhelm our students, students can use knowledge stored in long-term memory to "cheat" these limitations (Christodoulou, 2014). To illustrate this idea, let's return to the food delivery example.

Suppose there were six complex orders to place over the phone, but you had already memorized two of them (i.e. because you already knew your order and Stephanie always orders the same thing). In this instance, there would only be four *new* orders to hold in working memory as you placed the order, with two of them coming from long-term memory. While the four new orders will still impose a load on working memory, the two familiar orders that are available from long-term memory will have minimal impact on the cognitive load involved in placing the order.

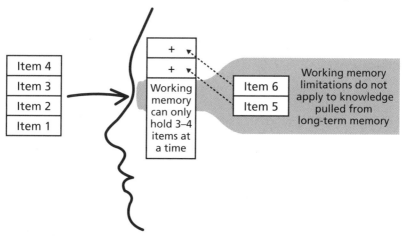

Figure 3: While too much incoming information will overload working memory, cognitive overload is prevented when students have prior knowledge on the topic

In essence, when our students have the right knowledge resources in their long-term memories, the cognitive load of tasks reduces (see Figure 3). While for a novice student 668 × 886 will impose a heavy load on working memory, when the student knows 6 × 8 by heart, as well as a firm grasp of the concepts and procedures involved in the multiplication algorithm, 668 × 886 can be solved effortlessly in seconds.

This neat trait of our cognition doesn't just apply to math or food delivery, but for pretty much everything we expect students to learn at school. For instance, when I give you the two texts in Table 1, the ease that you're able to understand and retain the meaning is highly dependent on the contents of your long-term memory.

Text A	Text B
The architecture of a CNN consists of several layers, such as convolutional, pooling, dropout, and fully connected layers, that process the input images and extract features. The loss function measures how well the network predicts the correct labels for the images. The optimizer updates the network parameters to minimize the loss. The training loop iterates over the training data, feeds it to the network, computes the loss and gradients, and applies the optimizer step.	At your PLCs, you will be identifying Tier 2 and Tier 3 accommodations for students with 504 plans and IEPs, including how you will utilize our PBIS acknowledgement system in accordance with our SIP plan. ECAs will be taking place in the gym at the same time, so we will meet in the MPR instead. It is explicitly stated in the CBA that at least one member of SLT and one member of SPED participates in each PLC. APs and ICs: please take notes and circulate to help with this process.

Table 1: Unless you are an expert in convolutional neural networks, your working memory will be heavily taxed by text A. By contrast, if you are an American educator, the acronym-dense text in text B should impose a lighter cognitive load

What does this "cognitive architecture" consisting of a limited working memory and an unlimited long-term memory imply for teaching? According to cognitive load theory, it is unreasonable to assume that students can just pick up the material as they go. The mind isn't a sponge, after all. Students have this bottleneck constraint called working memory that malfunctions when overloaded with unnecessary and excessive amounts of information. Effective teaching requires an understanding of these cognitive principles to design instruction that aligns with how the mind processes and stores information. Who but their teacher is better positioned to design instruction so that only the essential information is emphasized, and the unnecessary information is reduced or eliminated?

As someone who took pride in his classroom being busy and active, it was a hard pill to swallow that perhaps, just perhaps, all the "productive buzz" that my students were making was masking that they were overwhelmed, thinking about the wrong things, and making little progress. If I wanted my students to learn effectively and efficiently, I would need to change my approach. But which approaches were supported by cognitive science?

THE WORKED EXAMPLE EFFECT

The missing ingredient in "discovery" and "inquiry-based" classrooms like mine is **direct instructional guidance** (Kirschner et al., 2006). Rather than consuming students' limited working memories with trying to figure out unfamiliar material, teachers need to fully explain concepts to allow for focused processing on a small number of things at a time. Only when learners have successfully integrated the target skill or knowledge into long-term memory should teachers begin to remove scaffolds to allow for independent work.

Perhaps the most compelling evidence of the importance of direct instructional guidance comes to us from the abundance of studies demonstrating the **worked example effect**. In these studies, researchers would randomly divide students into two groups and give them a pre-test to ensure they didn't already know the material. Then, they would give Group 1 a series of problems to solve (see Table 2).

Group 1: Only problems	Group 2: Worked examples + problems
$$\frac{1}{5} + \frac{3}{4}$$ $$= ?$$	$$\frac{1}{5} + \frac{3}{4}$$ $$= \frac{1 \times 4}{5 \times 4} + \frac{3 \times 5}{4 \times 5}$$ $$= \frac{4}{20} + \frac{15}{20}$$ $$= \frac{19}{20}$$

Table 2: On the left is a problem without any steps explained, and on the right is a worked example that fully explains how to tackle this sort of problem

Group 2, however, would have half of their problems replaced with **worked examples** that explicitly taught them how to solve the problems. A worked example is a step-by-step illustration of how to carry out a task or solve a problem (see the right side of Table 2). Math teachers all over the world can be found using worked examples when they model mathematics procedures on the whiteboard. In English language arts, a worked example may come in the form of teacher-provided definitions and explanations after each line of a challenging text (Oksa et al., 2010). Expository diagrams, teacher "think alouds," instructional videos, and physically demonstrating processes for students are all manifestations of worked examples. The key feature of a worked example is that the material is fully explained (as opposed to a weak hint or a probing question) to the student.

The worked example "effect" is the finding that instruction without worked examples increases cognitive load and impairs learning, compared to instruction containing a generous supply of worked examples. It is simply more effective and more efficient to explain new material to novice students, and evidence suggests it will make students feel better about their learning, too (Mesghina et al., 2023).

The superiority of direct instructional guidance over minimal guidance makes total sense when we return to human cognitive architecture.

1. We know that working memory is easily overwhelmed when processing new and unfamiliar information. Fully explaining material to students takes away the burden of having to make a bunch of guesses and test a bunch of things out from an almost unlimited pool of possible combinations. Directly teaching the material helps them to process just the relevant information and reduces the mental processing associated with figuring out the material.

2. We know that long-term memory is unlimited, and that we use prior knowledge from long-term memory to think critically, creatively, and effectively. Fully explaining the material to students gives them resources *to think with* as they carry out future tasks. By contrast, we can predict that students will struggle and fail whenever we assign them tasks that assume knowledge and skills that they don't yet have.

When I first encountered the worked example effect, I had no argument to refute it, and when I searched the research databases of my university during my PhD, I couldn't find evidence that overturned it. Worked examples – full, explicit, explanations – help learning, and contrary to what I'd been told in teacher school, the absence of them hinders it.

EXPLAIN WITH UNDIVIDED ATTENTION: SET THE CONDITIONS FOR FOCUS

Here's a provocation: None of the recommendations that form the rest of this book will work if your students aren't listening.

Admittedly, the competition for students' attention is fierce. There's the rattle of the broken air-conditioner and the ticking of the clock. *Is it time to go yet? My shoes are wet. I'm hungry. Who's picking me up today?* There's the hidden social dynamics between friends and frenemies, which are amplified by the phones in their pockets. *Are people texting about me? There was a fight this morning that nobody told me about.* There are the constant disruptions from the same two students compounded by the ill-timed announcements over the PA system.

As teachers, we must be painstakingly meticulous in how we gain attention, sustain attention, and eradicate distractions from the learning environment. The more our students' precious, precious working memory space is occupied by things that are irrelevant or unrelated to what they're supposed to be learning, the fewer mental resources are available for dealing with the demands of the material (see Figure 4).

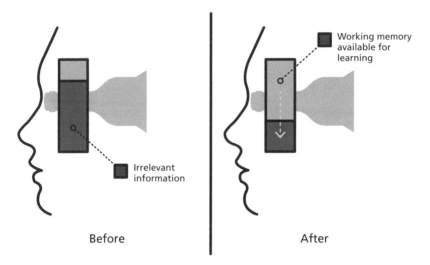

Working memory available for learning

Irrelevant information

Before   After

Figure 4: When we design instruction so that irrelevant information is minimized, working memory is freed up to deal with the things we need students to learn

To maximize the impact of an explanation, we have to ensure students are listening to it, and this involves eliminating anything (within our control) that has the potential to interfere with learning. To paraphrase explicit instruction expert Dr. Anita Archer, when teachers "cut the fluff," we free up working memory space so that students have a chance at learning "the stuff" they are being taught.

One major category of distraction is **attention-grabbing stimuli** in the learning environment. If a teacher places a dancing dog .gif in the first slide of their PowerPoint presentation, the students will inevitably concentrate on the dog rather than on what the teacher is saying (Pink & Newton, 2020). The same goes for busy classroom displays. Figure 5 shows four classrooms, two of which are crammed to the brim with eye-catching displays and decorations, while the other two are clearly much less busy.

Figure 5: When classrooms are highly decorated, time-on-task and learning decrease compared to more "plain" classrooms.

When researchers compare "busy" classrooms to classrooms that are more "plain," the students in the highly decorated classrooms tend to be more distractible and less learning takes place (Fisher et al., 2014). When learning scientists have studied the impact of highly decorated classrooms over time, they find similar negative effects on attention and learning, even when the same decorations are posted in the classroom for as long as 15 straight weeks (Godwin et al., 2022). The students don't seem to get accustomed to them.

The fact that classroom decorations can sometimes come with a penalty on attention and learning can be quite unsettling for those of us who value our classroom displays. However, in my view, if you like them – and designing them isn't sucking up planning time that could be going toward something more valuable – feel free to keep making them. Just try to make them less eye-catching and place them out in the hallway, or in a corner of the room that is out of view. That way, when you deliver your explanations, students will attend to what you are saying rather than looking past you to the contents of the display.

✓ Reduce visual clutter in the classroom environment.
✓ Place classroom displays away from where you're explaining.

But it isn't just busy classroom displays that teachers should be concerned about. Research on auditory distractions (e.g. Vasilev et al., 2018) suggests that noise harms learning. In one classic study conducted in New York City, students in classrooms that were adjacent to a noisy subway line learned significantly less than classrooms on the quiet side of the school (Bronzaft & McCarthy, 1975). Even background music, especially songs that contain lyrics, can make studying harder and less effective than if the studying takes place in silence (Perham & Currie, 2014). Why? Because students' working memories become occupied with thinking about their favorite songs, or the subway train, rather than the material they are supposed to learn. Despite the extensive evidence demonstrating that excessive noise is distracting, annoying, and harmful to learning (Caviola et al., 2021; Massonnié et al., 2022), many schools continue to construct open-plan classrooms that generate a lot of noise (Rance et al., 2023).

✓ Insist on silence in the classroom while you are explaining.
✓ Shut the door and close the partition when you are explaining.

Also, let's be honest. For most teachers, the majority of classroom distractions aren't generated by displays or poor architectural design. They're generated by the children. Research confirms the obvious: students become less attentive when surrounded by peers who distract them (Forrin et al., 2021). The most effective teachers are the "with-it" teachers; those who respond immediately to disruptive behavior (Brophy, 1986). We also know that teachers need to use *proactive* classroom management to prevent disruption from occurring (Kern & Clemens, 2007). Some important "antecedent strategies" that prevent disruption include the following:

1. Establish clear classroom rules and expectations.
2. Increase predictability in the environment.
3. Praise appropriate behavior.

4. Present material that is appropriately matched to student instructional level.

5. Use a brisk pace of instruction.

6. Provide a high number of opportunities to respond.

7. Use eye contact and proximity.

8. Arrange classroom seating to maximize attention.

How students enter the learning space can make or break a lesson. In elementary schools, I advise teachers to walk their students to class in a straight line, stopping on occasion to correct student behavior and remind students of the expectation for "voice-level zero" in the hallway. Before the students enter the classroom, the teacher should "frontload" the expectation that students will take their seats, keep their hands to themselves and have their eyes on the board, ready to learn from the teacher. In secondary schools, teachers should stand at the doorway and greet each student and do what I call a "transfer of energy" by reminding them with a warm but serious tone that they are now entering a space of rigorous learning. For all ages, students will sometimes need to "try it again" by exiting the classroom and reentering quietly and calmly if the expectation is not followed the first time.

Some schools, including those I have worked with on behavior, will increase predictability by having every lesson start with a "Do Now." In every room, and every class period, the expectation is to come in, retrieve your materials from the same place, and get started right away on the task on the board. Such a system, which also includes rewards for students who complete their work in silence and consequences for students who slip, ensures that the conditions are set for teachers to teach.

One of the lowest hanging fruit to prevent persistent disruption is to make a seating plan. Children should be seated so that they are facing the source of information: the teacher and the board. Rows (and, in elementary, numbered dots on the carpet) allow the teacher to scan the room and make eye contact with each and every one of their students. Frustratingly, many teachers have been led to believe that their students will be more engaged if they are sat in arrangements in which half of the students are unable to see the board without craning their neck or turning around each time the teacher is talking.

Providing students with an assigned seat via a seating chart is also important. Just as a child will choose candy over broccoli if given the option, many students will choose to sit in the back of the class so they can lay low, and next to their friends so they can socialize. It is showing empathy – not cruelty – to assign students to the seat that maximizes their attention, not least because it relieves them from the immense social pressure of having to choose between friends and learning.

> ✓ Use proactive behavior management strategies to create an environment that is conducive for attention.
> ✓ Arrange classroom seating so that students are facing away from their friends and toward the teacher.

Of course, I'm not suggesting that teachers begin isolating students into office cubicles and depriving them of sunlight on the off chance a butterfly passes by a window. But we need to design for attention. Any element of the classroom that distracts, disrupts, or signals to students that paying attention isn't required or valuable needs to be scrutinized. Fostering the importance of listening should be a core value in the classroom. Too often, teachers sabotage themselves by apologizing for having to explain stuff. "Sorry guys, but I've got to talk at you for a bit. Don't worry, as soon as I'm done, the fun part begins." This is nothing but an invitation to tune out of the lesson until further notice. Ultimately, teachers need to lay the groundwork for explanation by developing a classroom culture that relishes the opportunity to learn from their teacher.

To close this chapter, I will go out on a limb and say that anything short of a school-wide ban of cellphones during lessons is a dereliction of duty. Cell phones interrupt, distract, and occupy the minds of our youth (OECD, 2023). Anyone who has worked in a challenging school knows that the students are not using them as encyclopedias and calculators, but to bully each other, exchange pornographic images, and organize fights and vaping parties in the bathrooms. They are not only awful for physical and mental health (Daniyal et al., 2022), but they interfere with attention when they are allowed into the learning environment (Ward et al., 2017).

In my personal experience with implementing cell phone bans, the process for banning them school-wide is easy and straightforward. First you gather teachers, and you tell them that starting next week we are a phone-free school. If we see it, we take it. Then you gather the students and tell them that we are now a phone-free school. If we see it, we take it. Then you tell the parents that we will be taking their child's phone if we see it. That is nonnegotiable, just as it is not up for discussion whether we allow toys, vapes, or nudity at school. You may have some parents who throw a fuss. Too bad. When you set it up so that every teacher, student, and parent knows that phones are guaranteed to be confiscated on sight, the phones will vanish. Children do not want their phones taken away. In one school I worked at with 750 children, we started by confiscating around 30 on the first day (teacher calls an administrator to come pick it up, where it is stored in the office), which reduced to around one or two a day for the rest of the year. Other schools have opted to use phone pouches and phone jails instead of the "If we see it, we take it" policy. It does not especially matter. It's your school's duty to ban them, and yours to follow that ban to the letter.

✓ Ban cell phones and don't look back.

Do I still have your attention? Good.

Now that your students have calmly entered your uncluttered classroom, proceeded to their assigned seats with their phones stored in their lockers or backpacks, and have been diligently working on the Do Now on the board, signal for their attention. *Insist* that all pencils are down, and all eyes are on you.

It's now time to teach.

EXPLAIN CLEARLY: SAY ONLY THE WORDS THAT NEED TO BE SAID

One of the least helpful things you can say to someone who is trying to improve their explanations is, "Try being clearer." If they knew how to be clearer, they would have done so. Nobody is trying to make their speech patterns unclear on purpose.

Besides, what does "be clearer" actually mean? Fortunately for us, there is a wealth of research on **teacher clarity** (Titsworth et al., 2015) that helps to bring, well, clarity to this important topic. When we stick to the point, and trim common but unproductive features from our speech, learning becomes much more straightforward for students.

VAGUENESS

Unclear explanations are, in part, characterized by imprecise, ambiguous, and uncertain sets of words (Serki & Bolkan, 2023). Researchers call these **vagueness** terms, and their mere presence make it hard to follow the train of thought of the speaker. The following excerpt contains several examples of vagueness terms, in bold, from a lesson reported by Smith and Land (1981):

> *This mathematics lesson* **might** *enable you to understand a* **little more** *about* **some things** *we* **usually** *call number patterns.* **Maybe** *before we get to* **what is likely** *the main idea of the lesson, you should review* **a few** *prerequisite concepts.* **Actually,** *the first concept you need to review is positive integers.* **As you probably know,** *a positive integer is any whole number greater than zero.*

This example might seem artificially vague, but you get the point. Researchers consistently find that students' cognitive load is reduced, and learning and satisfaction are improved, when these sorts of vagueness terms are excluded from speech (Serki & Bolkan, 2023; Titsworth et al., 2015). Figure 6 nicely illustrates the difference between teaching that is highly vague compared to teaching where only the essential information is included.

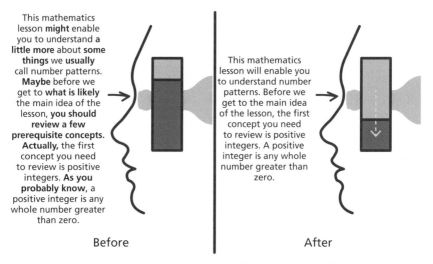

Before   After

Figure 6: Learning becomes much more straightforward when teachers prevent vague and uncertain language from creeping into their presentations

Vagueness terms can enter our speech when we're unconfident with the material, often because it is our first time teaching it. A simple strategy I use to address this issue is to practice my explanation in advance of teaching. I spend a little time modeling the material to an empty classroom, or to my wife or to a mirror. I've been known to practice explaining the material in the shower and in the car on the way to school.

Rehearsing teaching helps me to identify the most economical route for explaining something so that it's understood. With each additional rehearsal opportunity, my explanations become less vague and more coherent. If you don't believe me, consider how much the clarity of your teaching improves after teaching the same lesson (i.e. in middle or high school) six times in one day.

✓ Use precise language rather than ambiguous or vague terms.

✓ Rehearse explanations in advance of teaching.

MAZES

Just as the twisting corridors of a hedge maze prevent a direct path to freedom, so **mazes** interrupt the clear flow of speech from teacher to student. Mazes are what teacher clarity researchers call false starts, unnecessary repetitions, and hesitations, and it's been observed that, on average, about four mazes are committed for every one minute of teacher talk (Smith & Land, 1981). Notice how difficult it is to follow the paragraph on the left in Figure 7, which contains a dizzying array of halts, "uhs," and redundant sets of words, compared to when the mazes are cut, as in the paragraph on the right.

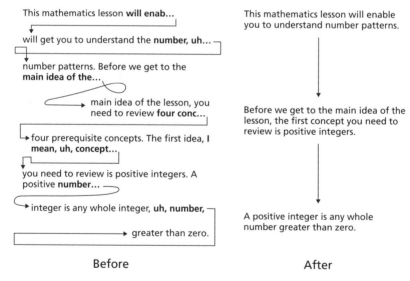

Before	After

Figure 7: Mazes are another form of disfluency in speech that can impose a load on limited working memory

Some of the most common mazes are "uh," "um," and their close cousin, "like." In many cases, these words are simply bad habits that will disappear once the speaker is made aware of them. One tried-and-true method I've used to help myself (and other teachers) with mazy, unclear explanations is to set up a tripod and record myself teaching. While it was at first a bit embarrassing to watch myself umming and uhhing through a presentation, it's allowed me to reflect and be intentional about the unproductive features of my speech and instructional delivery.

✓ Speak confidently and directly, avoiding false starts, hesitations, and unnecessary repetitions.

✓ Use video recordings to identify unproductive features of your speech.

DISCONTINUITY

Discontinuity happens when the speaker digresses from the logical flow of the lesson to interject information (Titsworth et al., 2015; Smith & Cotten, 1980). The interjected information might be totally irrelevant to the lesson, or is relevant but said at the wrong time. Table 3 provides an example of each type of discontinuity, in bold:

Irrelevant to the lesson	Relevant, but inappropriate timing
"Everyone have a look at this Venn diagram. We use Venn diagrams to compare and contrast information. **John Venn must have been a smart man for creating such an elegant diagram.** The similarities go in the middle of a Venn diagram, and the differences go on the outsides."	"Everyone have a look at this Venn diagram. We use Venn diagrams to compare and contrast information. **Tomorrow, you will not be working with Venn diagrams, but with cause and effect charts.** The similarities go in the middle of a Venn diagram, and the differences go on the outsides."

Table 3: Both instances of discontinuity interrupt the transition from one idea to the next with something else for students to think about

As subtle as the examples in Table 3 might seem, unnecessary or untimely information makes it more challenging to focus on the important parts of the explanation. Ideas in a presentation typically need to be thought about in relation to the rest of the ideas. Interrupting the smooth transition between ideas with an irrelevant interjection can interfere with the learner's cognitive processing.

One way to avoid discontinuous explanations is to plan lessons around a learning target or objective. When we have a well-defined goal for what students should be able to do as a result of instruction, it becomes much more obvious which information will help students to reach that goal, and which is unhelpful or unrelated. In the case of the examples in Table 3, we don't want students coming away with an appreciation of John Venn or cause and effect charts; we want them to be able to use a Venn diagram.

✓ Maintain a coherent thread from one idea to the next.
✓ Identify a lesson objective and stick to it.

SEDUCTIVE DETAILS

We can all remember a teacher who was famous for going off on tangents during their lessons. For me, this was a high school science teacher we'll call Mr. Sissom. Mr. Sissom loved to tell an old yarn or two about his farm. If there was even the slightest connection to be made to a farm story – such as a bee flying into the classroom – he would immediately launch into a dramatic retelling of the time he successfully eradicated a colony of wasps wearing only flip flops and a tank top. It didn't take long before his students began to catch on that if they simply interrupted the lesson to ask Mr. Sissom a farm-related question, they'd successfully get out of at least 20 minutes of biology class.

This brings us to the final type of information that compromises the clarity of our explanations: **seductive details**. Seductive details are defined as interesting or entertaining information that diverts student attention away from what they are supposed to be learning (Mayer, 2017). To illustrate, let's return to that lesson about how to fill in a Venn diagram. Sensing the material might be a bit dull for his students, Mr. Nguyen decides, on the fly, to spice up his lesson with some details that he knows will get young students laughing:

> *Everyone have a look at this Venn diagram. We use Venn diagrams to compare and contrast information.* **Yes, I know Venn diagrams look a lot like a butt. Once you see it, you can't get it**

out of your head! Anyway, *the similarities go in the middle of a Venn diagram, and the differences go on the outsides.*

Anyone with knowledge of young children will realize that it's exceptionally hard to get students to concentrate on academic content when butts are on the menu. The same goes for details that are "arousing" or "exciting." In one famous series of experiments, researchers divided participants into two groups and had them engage in an online lesson about lightning storm formation (Mayer et al., 2001). The difference between the groups was that the seductive details group was given access to short video clips showing lightning striking trees and the victims of lightning strikes being carried out on stretchers. As you probably predicted, the seductive details group significantly underperformed the group that received a lesson which only included the science content.

While school can use a bit of fun here and there, we should be careful about allowing fun to take over our lessons. My rule of thumb for including humor and tangential information in my lessons is pretty simple: always in moderation and, whenever possible, in service of learning.

✓ Allow the humor within the content to surface without forcing it.

✓ Only tell stories that help students to understand the material.

As we've seen, research into teacher clarity provides us with helpful guidelines and constraints that can be used to improve our explanations. When we cut unproductive features from our speech, such as vague and mazy sets of words, and avoid going off on tangents and diversions that occupy students' minds in lieu of the material, students will learn more and be more satisfied with our lessons. By using strategies such as practicing explanations in advance of teaching, watching videos of ourselves explaining, and aligning explanations with the objective of our lessons, we get several steps closer to mastering the art of explaining "clearer."

EXPLAIN INTERACTIVELY: ALTERNATE BETWEEN INPUTS AND OUTPUTS

As we discussed toward the start of this book, the worked example effect is a thing. It states that learning is enhanced when students have new and tricky material fully explained to them (Renkl, 2002; Sweller, 2006). However, this does not imply, as is often suggested by critics of explicit forms of teaching, that the entirety of our lessons should be dominated by continuous lecturing.

While students need heavy guidance during knowledge acquisition, they can also become overloaded if presented with too much information at once. One of the most common teaching blunders that I see in classrooms is when teachers provide their students with 11 pieces of essential information before giving them a multipart assignment that requires them to use that information. The teacher cannot know which of the 11 pieces were understood by the students (because they did not ask), and they can't even know which of the 11 were attended to (because they did not check.) The result is that the "extended lecture teacher" will experience nearly as much frustration as the "discovery teacher" when their students are unable to complete assignments as intended, and the material will end up needing to be re-explained.

THE ALTERNATING PRINCIPLE

Effective explainers, on the other hand, manage attention, behavior, and cognitive load by breaking their presentations down into smaller chunks (J. L. M. Smith et al., 2016). Then, to get students to adequately process each of those smaller chunks, they provide opportunities for students to rehearse and practice that information before moving on. The **alternating principle** (Pomerance et al., 2016; see Figure 8) is one of several names for the procedure of interspersing clear and concise teacher "inputs" with frequent student "outputs." These can include verbal responses (such as choral response or turn and talks) and written responses (such as through guided notes or mini whiteboards) (Heward & Wood, 2015).

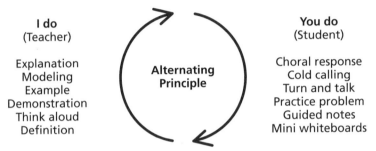

Figure 8: Effective explainers alternate between showing a small amount of information and checking students can successfully apply or revoice the information before moving on.

EXAMPLE/PROBLEM PAIRS

This "I explain a bit, you do something with it" instructional strategy is also referred to as **example/problem pairs,** based on the research into the worked example effect. In most of these studies, students are first provided with a step-by-step example of how to solve the problem, followed by a nearly identical problem for the learner to solve (van Harsel et al., 2021). Then back and forth they go through a series of pairs of worked examples that "push" the information in, and problems that "pull" the knowledge out (see Figure 9).

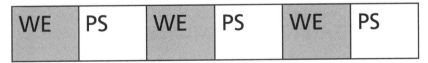

WE = Worked example
PS = Problem to solve

Figure 9: Example/problem pairs

While there is no hard and fast rule for how long a teacher should talk without eliciting a student response, effective explaining should look closer to the pattern found on the tennis court – a "serve and return" pattern – than that of the archery range. In the highly successful Direct Instruction (DI) programs, the rule of thumb is that students should be responding at a rate of around 9-12 responses per minute (achieved largely through choral response) during the early stages of acquiring a new skill. As the complexity of the material increases and the responses shift to being more individual and elaborative (i.e. "Is this fraction more than one?" → "How do you know whether a fraction is more than one?"), the response rate will concomitantly decrease (Watkins & Slocum, 2003).

All this is to say, effective explanation is not a monologue. It is dialogic. It is interactive. The teacher and the students *take turns*. To illustrate the "serve and return" approach to explaining, consider the following social studies lesson, in which the teacher briskly alternates between providing 1) information and 2) a chance for her students to rehearse each component of the information through a combination of choral responses, turn and talks, and hands-up cold calling.

Teacher: This is a Nile perch (*points to screen*). It is a type of fish.

What is a Nile perch, Class? (*signals for choral response*).

A type of fish!

Teacher: That's right. It is a type of fish. Even though it looks harmless, the Nile perch is a predator. It eats other fish and shrimp. In fact, when the Nile perch was first introduced to Lake Victoria, it drove hundreds of species of animals to extinction. It ate them all up. In just a few years, the Nile perch had eaten many of the native species in Lake Victoria.

Now I want you to turn and talk: What happened to Lake Victoria when the Nile perch was introduced?

Students immediately begin to talk. As the response will be short, the teacher stands in place rather than circulating, craning her neck back and forth to monitor behavior.

Teacher: Wrap up your discussions in 3, 2, 1 … all hands should be up. Proud and straight in the air.

⟳ What happened to Lake Victoria when the Nile perch was introduced … (*pauses*) … Bobby?

⟳ The Nile perch ate almost all the other animals, shrimp, fish. Soon it was one of the only fish.

Teacher: Excellent, Billy.

⟳ And where did this happen, Class? (*signals for choral response*).

⟳ Lake Victoria!

Teacher: That's correct! The Nile perch is a predator that drove many animals to extinction.

⟳ Class, they were almost driven to what? (*signals for choral response*).

⟳ Extinction.

Teacher: But there were two main benefits of introducing the Nile perch for the people of Lake Victoria. Number 1: The Nile perch became an important source of food for the people of Lake Victoria. Number 2: The Nile perch helped generate money for fishermen, who sold them in the market.

⟳ Now I want you to turn and talk: what were the two benefits of introducing the Nile perch?

⟳ *A buzz of student talk fills the room. Again, the teacher stands in place rather than circulating, this time leaning forward, a bit exaggeratedly, with her hand to her ear to convey to students she is listening in.*

Teacher: Wrap up your discussions in 3, 2, 1 … all hands should be up. Proud and straight in the air.

⟳ What were the two benefits of introducing the Nile perch? … (*pauses*) … Andrea?

⟳ The people ate the Nile perch, and the fishermen sold them for money.

Teacher: Excellent, Andrea. Isn't this fascinating, class? A negative of having the Nile perch introduced to Lake Victoria was that they ate many of the native species, but two benefits were that the Nile perch also provided much-needed food and money to the people of Lake Victoria.

✓ Explain in small steps, with each step followed by opportunities for students to respond.

✓ Ask questions to check that students are listening to and understanding your explanation.

ALL TOGETHER NOW: RESPONDING IN UNISON

Alternation serves several functions for teacher and students. For one, it helps to sustain student attention (MacSuga-Gage & Gage, 2015). Experiments that alter the volume of active student responses show that this improves focus and on-task behavior (Heward & Wood, 2015), as students learn to expect they will be called upon regularly. Student responses also provide formative data to the teacher on whether their explanation has flopped or landed successfully. The challenge then, for teachers, is not only to increase the number of student responses, but also to get students to respond in unison so that they don't copy each other's answers. There are two main unison response systems that I find tick all of these boxes: choral response and mini whiteboards.

CHORAL RESPONSE

If I could implement one instructional technique across all classrooms on this great earth, it would be choral response. This low-cost strategy allows me to check that my students are listening, while simultaneously collecting short-form feedback on my teaching from all 30 students at once. Table 4 gives an example of choral response in action.

I do	You do	I do	You do
Teacher: Here is a map of Spain. *Pauses to trace finger around Spanish borders.*	Teacher: Now class, tell me this country's name in 3, 2, 1 ... Students: Spain!	Teacher: That's right! And right in the middle is the Spanish capital, Madrid. *Signals with finger toward Madrid.*	Teacher: Now class, what is the capital of Spain? 3, 2, 1 ... Students: Madrid!

Table 4: Choral response

As in the example above, choral response is well suited for simple answers, such as yes/no and single words and numbers, but it can also be used for longer strings of words. For example, when teaching the concept of "equals 1" in a fractions lesson, I might ask, "A fraction that equals one has what, Class?" and prompt the students to say "The same number of parts on the bottom and the top" in unison. I've personally found the following guidelines for embedding choral response to be helpful and straightforward:

1. **Model the expectation** – Act out the roles of teacher and student for a couple of simple questions, and then practice with students. For example: "What is my name?" [pause briefly, give signal for students to respond]. "Dr. Groshell."

2. **Provide a brief thinking pause** – Let the complexity of the question determine the duration of the pause. If a question requires more than four or five seconds for students to answer, break the content into smaller chunks.

3. **Use a signal for students to respond** – The signal could be a finger snap or lowering your hand down. Saying "Class" and "Get ready" before signaling the students' response promotes unison responding.

4. **Provide feedback** – Confirm and/or praise immediately when hearing 100% correct answers. When one or two incorrect responses are heard, confirm the correct answer and repeat the question in a future part of the lesson. When more than a few incorrect responses are heard, state the correct answer along with a brief explanation and immediately repeat the question, followed by a choral response.

5. **Mix in cold calling** – Now and then, instead of signaling a choral response, call on an individual student. Present the question *before* calling a randomly selected student's name so that all students must think about the question and nobody can predict when they will be called on.

6. **Maintain a brisk pace** – Alternating at a fast pace leads to more responses, higher accuracy, and less off-task behavior than teaching with a slower pace. Prepare questions prior to the lesson

to enable you to move without hesitation from one portion of the lesson to the next.

(Adapted from Twyman and Heward (2018))

Unfortunately in education, choral response is unfairly maligned. People will tell me that it "doesn't sit right" with them, or even compare it to dog training. This is when the prevailing approach in many classrooms is to allow the same students to repeatedly opt out of their learning. All it takes to recognize this is to sit in on a classroom and count the number of responses by the quietest and/or most disadvantaged students. By relying too much on traditional hands-up to encourage participation, the teacher ends up calling on the same handful of students throughout the lesson. These are often the highest achieving students; those who likely already knew the answers to the questions before the lesson began. By contrast, choral response allows the teacher to involve all 30 students *dozens of times per lesson* in a nonthreatening manner. The fact that it is executed swiftly, without taking out any equipment, makes it among the most cost-beneficial strategies available (Twyman & Heward, 2018).

✓ Increase the number of responses you elicit by having students respond in unison, rather than just one at a time.

✓ Teach at a brisk pace to increase the number of responses you can elicit per lesson.

MINI WHITEBOARDS

To be fair to the critics of choral response (who, let's be honest, have probably not given it the time of day it deserves), there are other strategies that get students responding in unison. Mini whiteboards are a whole class response tool that can be used to check and respond to student understanding of an explanation. Consider the example in Table 5 of a teacher using mini whiteboards to address a common regrouping error.

WE	PS	WE	PS
On her whiteboard, the teacher fully explains how to regroup a 10 into the 10s column and add it to the sum. 1 19 + 12 1 1 19 + 12 31	Students attempt a similar problem on their whiteboard. As is the class routine, all students hide their response against their body when they are done. 1 17 + 14 2 1	Teacher says "3, 2, 1 … show me," and scans the boards. Having seen a few errors, she swiftly works out the problem, highlighting where the error occurred. 1 17 + 14 1 1 17 + 14 31	Students attempt a new problem, this time getting it correct. 1 18 + 13 3 1

Table 5: Using mini whiteboards

By using the "3, 2, 1 … show me" routine, the teacher is able to determine who's getting it and who isn't, so she can determine the next steps in the lesson. This could be to reteach the material, as we saw above, or move on to the next part of the lesson. If the same students keep falling off the bus, the teacher can elect to meet with these students in a small group while the rest of the students are working on an independent task.

As with choral response, using mini whiteboards requires *all* students to think, participate, and feed back their understanding to the teacher *all at once*. A clear advantage of mini whiteboards is that they can be used for a variety of response types – not just single words or chains of words. The main drawbacks are that they must be taken out and then stored somewhere, and the markers have to be replenished. It's perhaps due to these reasons that in my experience so many teachers tend to reserve them for small group instruction and fun occasions (i.e. game show time!) rather than integrating them into whole group lessons. This is a shame, because they can be transformative for learning when paired with strong classroom management routines and a culture in which everyone participates.

✓ Check that each segment of your explanation has been understood by having students show you their answers on mini whiteboards.
✓ Evaluate student responses to determine when to explain again and when to forge ahead or differentiate.

ELICITING HARD THINKING

There are other active response techniques that do not achieve the 100% response rate, but that still elicit a high ratio of thinking and/or participation. These deserve to be in the explainer's toolkit because of the unique advantages they bring in certain instructional situations, the variety they bring to the learning experience, and the role they play in cultivating a more engaged and thoughtful classroom atmosphere. I will highlight three of these that work closely together: cold calling, think time, and turn and talk.

COLD CALLING

If there is one technique that draws the ire of non-teachers and faculties of education more than choral response, it is cold calling. In case you didn't already know, cold calling involves calling on a random student to answer a question rather than a volunteer. The procedure can be used to elicit longer responses than can typically be chanted or scribbled on a mini whiteboard, or to promote class discussion in which students elaborate on each other's answers. Here's an example:

Teacher: Class, here's a question for you.

 Describe the process by which plants make their own food using sunlight. Take a moment to think about it ... Get ready ... Okay, now all hands in the air, straight and proud.

Now ... Fatima, what's your answer?

Fatima: Plants use sunlight to convert carbon dioxide and water into glucose and oxygen. It's called photosynthesis.

A few things to note from this example of cold calling. First, the teacher started by asking the question to the whole class before saying Fatima's name. This contrasts with the more conventional ordering, in which the student's name is said before the question is posed (e.g. "Fatima, describe the process by which plants make their own food using sunlight"). Thus, while the class's overall response rate is lowered because only Fatima gets to say the answer, the teacher has achieved a high "think rate" by prompting all the students to consider the question.

Second, the teacher has incorporated think time into the questioning sequence (see the next section of this chapter). The answer is long, and requires retrieving and ordering multiple items from long-term memory in order to construct an answer. If the students have their notebooks out, the teacher could also have had the students write down their answer prior to cold calling.

Third, right before the teacher asks the question, she asks everyone to put their hands up. This is optional, but I'm convinced it leads to a higher success rate on the responses, as it makes it crystal clear that everyone is equally eligible to be called on.

Finally, it should be noted that cold calling has been practiced, justified, and normalized in this class. The culture of this class is that everyone thinks and everyone participates, because learning is that important. Cold calling isn't seen as a "gotcha," but an opportunity for students to share what has been adequately taught to them. I don't know about you, but I'd send my own children a million times over to a school that actively seeks the contributions of all students than to a school that only enlists the students who are willing to raise their hands.

Research on cold calling supports its positive impact. While it clearly enhances participation and engagement (Thulasidas & Gunawan, 2022), cold calling appears to improve the very outcomes that skeptics suggest it worsens. A couple of notable studies have shown that increasing cold calling does not make students more uncomfortable, but instead leads to increased *volunteering* in class discussions (Dallimore et al., 2013). While a gender gap emerges in low cold-calling environments, with women answering fewer questions than men, high cold-calling environments have been shown to lead to equal rates of participation between women and men (Dallimore et al., 2019). Furthermore, as cold calling helps to build schema through the same mechanisms as retrieval practice, evidence suggests that it can alleviate stress during learning, rather than heighten it (A. M. Smith et al., 2016).

✓ Pose questions to the whole class, then call the name of a non-volunteer.

THINK TIME

Think time, or "wait time," sits in this section of the chapter right after cold calling and before turn and talk, because it bolsters both techniques. When teachers pose a question to the whole class about the material that they have just explained, they should pause to allow everyone to think before prompting them to talk about it with a partner or picking a non-volunteer.

According to the available research on think time, the typical teacher pauses only about 0.7–1.4 seconds after their questions before eliciting student responses (Stahl, 1994). The pause tends to last even less time when teachers question students who are perceived as low ability. However, when teachers give clear and concise explanations followed by a pause that lasts a bit longer, e.g. at least three seconds, students tend to provide longer and more accurate responses with fewer "I don't know" responses, and their volunteering and learning increases (Stahl, 1994; Wasik & Hindman, 2018).

Think time is one of those tricky components of an effective explanation that can feel at odds with another important component: teaching at a brisk pace (Hughes et al., 2019). In my experience of working with teachers, the pacing almost always needs to be faster than what most teachers expect. Lessons that lag are invitations for students to tune out or misbehave. To calibrate their pacing, I recommend that teachers combine observations of off-task behavior with student error rate: A high rate of off-task behavior signals that the teaching may be too slow, while a high rate of student errors signals that the teaching may be too fast and/ or does not provide adequate think time after questions.

Cognitively, think time can be described as "covert" retrieval and mental rehearsal that serves as a bridge between answering a question or solving a problem "overtly" (Sumeracki & Castillo, 2022). One research-based strategy that is closely related to think time is to prompt students to construct a visualization of the material in their heads. I once had the pleasure of seeing this in action when I walked in on a class of kindergarten children who were eagerly asking to learn about tying shoes. Not wanting to miss out on a "teachable moment," the teacher proceeded to show everyone how to tie a shoe with her own shoelaces using the "bunny-ears" method. Then, instead of having the students jump straight to practicing the bunny-ears method on their own shoes, she had everyone close their eyes and visualize the steps that she had just demonstrated to them.

"Now that your eyes are closed," she said, "I want you to visualize the first step I showed you. Picture how I did it in your mind. Okay, now visualize the second step. If you need to, you can move your hands in the air to copy the step exactly as I did it. Okay, now visualize the third step."

Once she had given students some personal "think time," she prompted them to practice on their shoes. The "imagination" or "mental imagery" exercise served as an intermediary step between her worked example and the students' application of the worked example.

As is often the case, the teacher's instincts are backed by quite a bit of research (Fiorella & Mayer, 2016). In one study, the researchers provided the participants with a worked example on the steps for how to operate spreadsheet software (Sweller et al., 2011a). Then for their second task, one group of students was given another worked example, while the other was asked to imagine the steps of the previous worked example they had studied. Imagining the steps was found to be more effective for the learners who were secure after the first worked example than being provided a second worked example. In another study, the researchers coached a pianist to perform a visualization exercise in which she imagined herself playing a specific piece of music. Stunningly, the mental act of rehearsing the piece through visualization was shown to be a solid substitute for hands-on practice with a piano, with her performance on the piece actually improving (Christakou et al., 2019).

✓ Insert a pause of around three seconds before eliciting responses.

✓ Give students time to mentally rehearse and visualize the material that they are learning.

TURN AND TALK

Turn and talk is one of the techniques in this book that is hard to get right, but worth the investment. When managed well, it leads to a high think ratio in which 50% of students are actively responding, and 50% of students receive an additional explanation from their peer. One of my overcorrections during my transition away from progressive education was to shun turn and talk, aka think-pair-share, relegating it to the dustbin of romantic ideas that sound good in theory but rarely pay off in practice. Even as I endorse it now, I observe more terrible examples of turn and talk in classrooms than good ones. Where to begin?

1. The students aren't talking about the content. They're socializing.

2. The students are fake talking (muttering unintelligible sounds, smiling, nodding their heads) and only start talking when the teacher gets closer.

3. While one student is doing a good job of talking about the content, the other isn't listening.

4. Both students are talking at the same time, so neither is listening.

5. One student talks the whole time, so the other doesn't get a chance to talk.

6. One student refuses to work with their partner, so nobody is talking or listening.

7. A few students are absent that day, so the newly formed partners and the group of three are acting confused and not talking.

8. The teacher didn't explain the material fully, so the students don't know enough to be able to talk.

9. The question was confusingly worded, so everybody is staring blankly at each other, not talking.

10. The question required a one-word response (i.e. a number), so the turn and talk ends almost as soon as it started.

The reason that I say that turn and talk is worthwhile, despite all the pitfalls, is that it harnesses a mechanism that has been shown to facilitate learning: the **self-explanation effect**. Many researchers have investigated the effectiveness of prompting students to explain as a teaching technique (Bisra et al., 2018). In typical self-explanation studies, participants begin by studying the same instructional text, such as on the human circulatory system, before being randomly sorted into two groups. The first group is given self-explanation prompts such as, "Could you explain how the blood vessels work?" and an empty text box to provide their response to each question. The participants in the comparison group are only given an empty box for note taking. Participants who are prompted to explain the material tend to learn the material better than the participants who just take notes (Lin & Atkinson, 2013).

Of course, teachers could make use of self-explanation without having to resort to turn and talk, but each alternative comes with its own challenges. For many students, verbally explaining the material is much faster than putting it into writing. Self-explanation could also be facilitated through voice recordings, but this requires taking out 30 devices and students logging in to record simultaneously, and these recordings must be completed in a quiet place, away from other students, if anyone wants to have a shot at being able to hear the end product. Turn and talk, on the other hand, is highly efficient when designed well. The following are some guidelines for turn and talk influenced by Stewart and Swanson (2019):

Be intentional in the student pairings.

- Sit students next to their turn and talk partner, facing forward.
- Use a seating chart to ensure the best possible combination of partners.
- Seat struggling learners next to students who are supportive.
- Seat less proficient English language learners next to more proficient English language learners.

Assign A and B roles to each pair.

- Inform the students who is Partner A and who is Partner B. This can be done with labels on the desks.

- In some classrooms, the window and door can be used for A and B roles; students on the side of the window are Window partners, and students on the side of the door are Door partners.

Establish a consistent routine.

- Step 1: Explain the material to the students in full.
- Step 2: Ask the question. Pause for think time. Prompt Partner A to respond.
- Step 3: Partner A responds to the question while Partner B listens.
  - Use a timer so that partners get the same amount of talk time.
  - End with "Finish talking in 3, 2, 1 …"
- Step 4: Partner B elaborates on the question while Partner A listens.
  - After the timer goes off, use the class signal to regain student attention.
  - Cold call a student to share their answer or their partner's answer.

Teach the routine explicitly.

- Model the routine with a volunteer student.
- Have Partner A students and then Partner B students raise their hands to check that they know their role.
- Practice the routine with simple questions at first.
- Praise and reward good performance.

Teach additional considerations.

- When turning and talking, students must remember to:
  - Tell their partner the answer in one or two sentences.
  - Listen without interrupting while their partner talks.
  - Be prepared to share what their partner said.
  - Be kind and supportive so everyone feels comfortable sharing their answers.

When first rolling out a strong turn and talk routine, it is often necessary to stand in place at the front of the room to monitor the talking. Circulating the room signals to students that the only time you are watching them is when you are close by. Standing in the same spot the entire time and leaning forward and nodding your head, even if you can't really hear everything, conveys that you are listening in on what they are saying. Once your turn and talk routine has been going smoothly for a few weeks, you will want to walk to groups and listen in on their discussions so that you can collect formative data on student understanding.

Most importantly, the success of any given turn and talk is largely determined by how well the students know the material. Asking a student to explain material that they know nothing about is unlikely to bear much fruit (Clinton et al., 2016). You're going to have to explain it to them first and have them turn and talk about it second.

> ✓ Follow explanations with prompts that require students to explain the material in their own words.
> ✓ Have students turn and talk about what was just explained to them.

In this chapter, we've encountered several principles. Teachers should explain a small bit of information at a time and pause to check that students are getting it. Momentarily turning over the task to the students allows for adequate processing time of each element of the material, which serves to develop the long-term memory resources that they'll need to tackle future, more complex tasks. Since calling on individuals prevents the teacher from sampling the understanding of everyone in the room, as well as depriving other students of the opportunity to do the mental work of answering questions, teachers should seek to utilize techniques that require a high percentage of students thinking and responding at the same time. Examples include choral response, mini whiteboards, cold calling, think time, and turn and talks.

Among these insights, what are your main takeaways? Which of these could be a focus of yours for the next few weeks of teaching? Turn and talk to your partner about it and be prepared to share.

EXPLAIN WITH VISUALS: PAIR SPEAKING WITH IMAGES AND DRAWINGS

Speaking is perhaps mankind's greatest educational tool (Mayer, 2017), but it also has its limitations. For one, spoken words are a highly "transient" form of information, meaning that they tend to slip out of mind before the learner has time to adequately process them (Wong et al., 2019). To combat the negative effects of transience, the explainer must ensure that they are giving their audience sufficient processing time with each element of information that they are supposed to learn. As we discussed in the previous chapter, think time can be used to pause the unrelenting deluge of an explanation, and lectures can be broken up by asking questions and checking for understanding.

Another way to prevent explanations from going in one ear and out the other is to make the speech *permanent* through the use of visuals, such as images, diagrams, and graphics. Visuals provide a tangible anchor or reference point for the content being communicated, and they can be used to represent complex information in an organized manner (Caviglioli, 2019). When it comes to managing cognitive load, the use of visuals supports learning by tapping into a feature of working memory that we haven't covered so far.

According to **dual coding theory**, working memory is not a single processor, but consists of two separate and complementary "channels": the verbal system and the nonverbal (i.e. visual) system. Having these two channels enables us to efficiently process spoken and visual information simultaneously without inducing a double penalty on working memory.

To reflect the dual channels, let's go ahead and update our mental model (i.e. the wine bottle metaphor) of the learner in Figure 10.

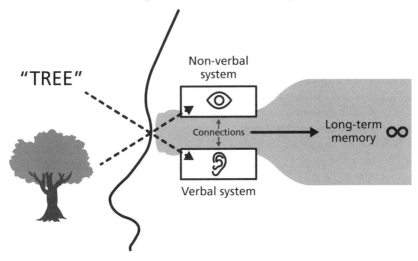

Figure 10: The dual channel assumption of working memory

As Figure 10 shows, when we encounter information in complementary modalities, such as hearing the word "tree" and seeing an image of a tree, the verbal system processes the linguistic aspects of the information (i.e. the meaning of the word) while the nonverbal system processes the sensory and perceptual aspects (i.e. the imagery) associated with the information. As the information is distributed across the two channels, the overall strain on working memory is reduced (Castro-Alonso & Sweller, 2020). Additionally, integrations and connections between the two representations are likely to be made, which enhances the overall strength and robustness of the memory trace in long-term memory.

Fortunately for educators, there is an abundance of research on designing visual presentations based on the **multimedia principle**: the finding that presentations are usually more effective when they include words *and* visuals, and not just words (Mayer, 2017). Table 6 contains a selection of the multimedia principles that seem especially pertinent to our discussion on improving explanations. I invite you to pay special attention to the column on the right, which describes why each principle is important for improving your explanations.

Name of principle	What to do	How it works and why it helps
Multimedia principle	Use words and visuals, not just words.	Images and diagrams help make the material more concrete by giving students a tangible representation of what you're saying.
Coherence principle	Exclude unnecessary visuals and words.	Unnecessary visuals and words eat up working memory capacity. They draw limited attention away from what the student is supposed to be learning.
Redundancy principle	Avoid displaying written text that repeats or duplicates what you're saying.	Learning is optimized when you speak and present images at the same time, but you risk overloading students when you display written text that says the same thing you're saying.
Signaling principle	Direct student attention to the parts of the presentation you want them to focus on.	Using your finger or a tool to point, circle, underline, or highlight helps guide the students' cognitive processing during a visual presentation.
Dynamic drawing principle	Draw on the board while speaking rather than referring to already drawn graphics.	Drawing as you speak allows you to direct student attention toward one piece of information at a time, something that is not possible with an already drawn graphic.

Table 6: Important multimedia principles for explaining

Because Table 6 contains a wealth of information, I should probably *show* you what each of the principles looks like by leveraging visuals to help support your understanding. Let me now take you through a tutorial of each of these principles, starting from the top of the table.

TUTORIAL OF MULTIMEDIA PRINCIPLES

THE MULTIMEDIA PRINCIPLE

If you've ever found yourself using an instruction manual, perhaps to put together an appliance or a piece of furniture, you will know that they often include a combination of words and visuals. Instructions without visuals force us to mentally construct images based on the inferences we draw from the printed words, which can be quite demanding for working memory. The same effect happens to students when teachers overlook the importance of visuals when modeling and explaining. For example, if a teacher were to use just words to explain how a bike pump works, the students would probably have a hard time picturing what the teacher is talking about. As mentioned above, this is the **multimedia principle**: Use words and visuals, not just words (Figure 11).

Speaking only
"When the handle is pushed up, the piston moves up, the inlet valve closes, the outlet valve opens, and air moves out through the hose."

Speaking with visuals
"When the handle is pushed up ..."

Figure 11: An explanation on how a bike pump works is enhanced when paired with supporting images

THE COHERENCE PRINCIPLE

However, it is important when designing presentations that we don't just throw in lots images for the sake of it. The same goes with words. Moreover, the images, graphics, and animations that teachers use need to *complement* the message of the explanation. Anything that is decorative or unrelated, as Figure 12 shows on the left side, should be excluded from presentations. This is the **coherence principle**: Exclude unnecessary images and words.

Figure 12: While the two extra images on the left are superficially related to bike pumps, they do not promote meaning making. If anything, they are a distraction

THE REDUNDANCY PRINCIPLE

Similarly, teachers should speak over a complementary visual, but avoid displaying words on the board that essentially say the same thing that they are communicating verbally. Redundant words in a presentation are a source of extraneous cognitive load, as students will be forced to read both the words on the board and listen to the teacher's narration at the same time (Albers et al., 2023); see Figure 13. Rather than using their slides as a script, teachers should hide redundant text (i.e. in the notes section of PowerPoint) to allow students to focus just on the words being said and the images being displayed. This phenomenon is called the **redundancy principle**: Avoid displaying written text that repeats or duplicates what you're saying.

Figure 13: By displaying written text that repeats what he's saying, the teacher on the left risks overloading his students

THE SIGNALING PRINCIPLE

Continuing down the list of multimedia principles in Table 6, teachers need to use their fingers or a tool to point, circle, underline, or highlight each piece of material as they explain it. Using visual and verbal cues to guide the students' cognitive processing during a presentation is known as the **signaling principle**: Direct student attention to the parts of the presentation you want them to focus on. Using a marker does the trick for whiteboards, and digital arrows and circles are easy to add into slides presentations. It's equally important to verbally call attention to each element of the material (e.g. "We should all have eyes on the board, tracking my finger, please"), as you explain.

Unsignaled	Signaled
"The outlet valve opens, and air moves out through the hose."	"The outlet valve opens, and air moves out through the hose."

Figure 14: The teacher on the right has circled the outlet valve and is signaling toward it with his finger, which helps students to pair his spoken words with the correct part of the diagram

THE DYNAMIC DRAWING PRINCIPLE

The final multimedia principle describes the finding that drawing each element of a graphic while speaking is often more effective than speaking over a completed graphic (Mayer et al., 2020). This makes sense when we combine many of the concepts from this book. Drawing lowers the cognitive load of a complex diagram by funneling one item of the diagram into working memory at a time, allowing teachers to pause, check for understanding, and signal toward each new item as they're added. This is called the **dynamic drawing principle**: Draw on the board while speaking rather than referring to already drawn graphics.

Already drawn

"The outlet valve opens, and air moves out through the hose."

Progressively drawn

"The outlet valve opens, and air moves out through the hose."

Figure 15: Drawing each component of the diagram from scratch helps to guide cognitive processing by limiting what is presented to one thing at a time.

When I present these principles to teachers, the top question I'm asked is whether I would suggest they stop using PowerPoints and simply draw on blank canvas. They ask this question to a presenter who is using PowerPoint slides to deliver his presentation. The truth is that it is possible to use animations in PowerPoint so that only one thing at a time is funneled into working memory. The trouble is that these animations are quite time-consuming, and some teachers find them challenging to use, so they don't do them.

PowerPoints are often more of a hindrance than helpful, as anyone who has been to a conference and seen the excessive amounts of text and grainy clipart can attest to. But among the benefits of a PowerPoint presentation is that it can be used year after year, and shared with colleagues. I recommend a hybrid of PowerPoint and drawing using a relatively unknown technique: Simply press B (for black) on your keyboard during a PowerPoint presentation to black out your slides when you don't want students looking at them. Then draw on the whiteboard to harness the power of the dynamic drawing principle.

✓ Select and use visuals that complement your explanations.

✓ Avoid adding visuals that could interfere with comprehension or clutter the presentation.

✓ Avoid putting excessive amounts of text on the board.

✓ Signal (point, circle, highlight) toward the parts of the presentation that you want students to focus on.

✓ Start with a blank canvas and progressively add information to the board as you explain.

EXPLAIN WITH EXAMPLES: SHOW WHAT IT IS AND WHAT IT ISN'T

What is the difference between an example and an explanation? **Examples** illustrate specific instances of the material. *This is glerm* and *This is not glerm*. They can be positive, providing a sample of what something is, or negative, providing a sample of what something is not. **Explanations** provide context and understanding by breaking down the concept. They don't just show what something is; they also reveal how it works or why it's relevant.

There are two main points I want to convey in this chapter. The first is that providing a single, positive example is rarely enough to teach a topic. The second is that, in addition to providing a series of carefully chosen examples and non-examples, teachers can use erroneous examples and analogies to further their students' understanding.

The classic example of the importance of carefully chosen examples comes from Engelmann and Carnine, the originators of the highly effective Direct Instruction (DI) programs (Engelmann & Carnine, 2016). Imagine a teacher stands at the front of the classroom and says, "This is glerm" while waving a green cloth over their head. This simple stimulus prompts the student to make inferences. It could be that glerm means "waving." It could also mean "cloth." It could also mean "above," "green," or a combination of these terms. Glerm could mean a lot of things, and it is only when the teacher rules out all other interpretations, that the students will be able to arrive at the correct meaning of glerm.

Providing students just one example is unlikely to help them to appreciate the full range of contexts or situations in which the concept applies, and it will often lead to misinterpretations. Consider for a moment how you might teach a Third grade lesson on symmetry (Figure 16).

Figure 16: A single (positive) example of how to draw a line of symmetry

You could provide Figure 16 and say, "This is how to draw a line of symmetry," before assigning a worksheet in which students are meant to draw their own dotted lines on a variety of shapes. I did this very thing when I taught Third grade, thinking the concept was just too obvious to require further elaboration. Of course, for a learner who is new to symmetry, the single example could be interpreted to mean, "Symmetry is drawing a dotted line down the middle of a shape" (see Figure 17).

Figure 17: The lack of variation in examples led this student to infer that drawing a line of symmetry is to "draw a dotted line down the middle of a shape"

Figure 17 is a perfectly reasonable, but incorrect, response by the students, given that the teacher provided only one example. The students need to be exposed to multiple examples to be able to appreciate that the line could be vertical, horizontal, or any which way, *and* it must result in the two halves of the shape being mirror images of each other. Otherwise, half your class will end up (as they did with me) drawing vertical lines down every shape on their worksheet, and you'll have to stop the whole thing to revise everyone's understanding.

In addition to providing too few examples, I commonly observe teachers presenting only *positive* examples of what is being taught without providing any non-examples. **Non-examples** provide a clear contrast to positive examples, allowing learners to discriminate between *what is* and *what is not* an instance of the concept being taught. Without non-examples, students are unlikely to develop an understanding of the variation within concepts (Ling Lo, 2012). Engelmann and Carnine developed a set of principles that teachers can use to systematically sequence examples and non-examples. While I'll continue to use the topic of symmetry, these principles can be used to present all sorts of material.

TUTORIAL OF PRINCIPLES FOR SEQUENCING EXAMPLES

THE WORDING PRINCIPLE

It is important when you are first exemplifying a concept to keep the same wording throughout (Watkins & Slocum, 2003): "This is an arch; this is not an arch" and "This is a bullying; this is not bullying." This small nuance in the **wording principle** helps to create an association between the example and the meaning, as well as keeping the teacher's speech as precise as possible. See Table 7 for an example. In later lessons, you'll gradually introduce more varied wording to add richness to the language surrounding the concept.

Following the wording principle	Not following the wording principle
This is a line of symmetry. This is not a line of symmetry.	This is a line of symmetry. This is asymmetrical.

Table 7: How to follow the wording principle

THE SET UP PRINCIPLE

To "set students up" for success, and to maximize efficiency, we really want to think about how we will use the fewest possible examples to demonstrate the concept. To minimize the number of examples needed for the **set up principle**, teachers should start by juxtaposing examples that share the greatest possible number of features (Watkins & Slocum, 2003). This forces students to attend to just the single feature, removing other possible interpretations. See Table 8 for an example. In later lessons, you'll gradually introduce more varied examples to further expand the range of the concept.

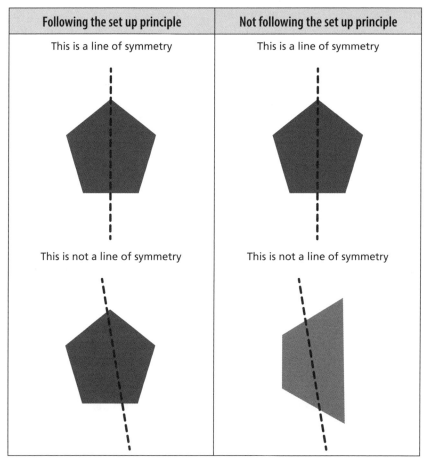

Following the set up principle	Not following the set up principle
This is a line of symmetry	This is a line of symmetry
This is not a line of symmetry	This is not a line of symmetry

Table 8: While the non-example on the right could eventually be used, the non-example on the left keeps the pentagon constant to allow the students to attend only to the drawing of the line.

THE DIFFERENCE PRINCIPLE

To illustrate the boundaries of a concept, teachers should juxtapose examples with non-examples that are just ever so slightly different, rather than providing non-examples that are quite a bit different. These "minimally different" juxtapositions are easier to process in mind, and avoid leaving interpretation to chance. As Table 9 shows, when the **difference principle** is employed, the students will know more or less the exact point in which a line of symmetry is no longer a line of symmetry when a minimal difference juxtaposition is presented.

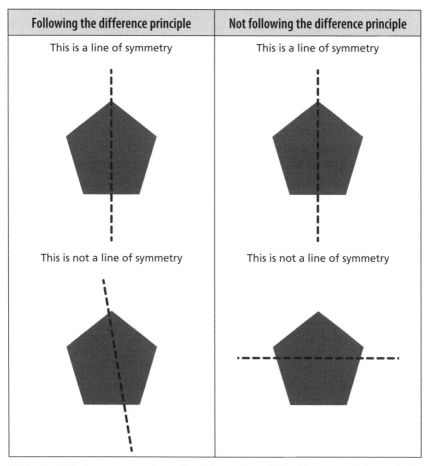

Following the difference principle	Not following the difference principle
This is a line of symmetry	This is a line of symmetry
This is not a line of symmetry	This is not a line of symmetry

Table 9: While the non-example on the right could, and should, eventually be used, the non-example on the left more precisely indicates exactly when the line of symmetry has no longer been correctly drawn.

THE SAMENESS PRINCIPLE

Following the previous principles goes a long way to illustrate symmetry, but it won't guarantee a complete understanding. If only purple shapes are used, students could infer that "lines of symmetry can only be drawn down purple shapes." If only polygons are used, students could infer that "a line of symmetry can only be drawn on polygons." For the **sameness principle**, as students gain understanding of the concept, teachers should begin to show the range of the concept by juxtaposing examples that differ from one another as much as possible and yet still illustrate the concept. Table 10 shows an example of a teacher who now begins to include non-polygonal figures in her example sequence. This sequence fosters generalization.

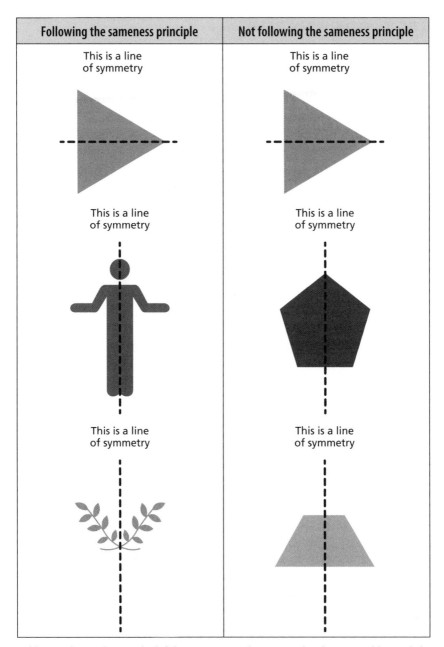

Following the sameness principle	Not following the sameness principle
This is a line of symmetry	This is a line of symmetry
This is a line of symmetry	This is a line of symmetry
This is a line of symmetry	This is a line of symmetry

Table 10: The teacher on the left begins to introduce examples that expand beyond the realm of polygons, to show students that the rule still applies to these figures.

THE TESTING PRINCIPLE

After a while, you will have illustrated an extensive range of possibilities of the concept, including other critical features of symmetry I've not mentioned (e.g. that you can't draw a line of symmetry on shapes that are not symmetrical). Imagine you're at the point in the sequence where you've taught everything in Figure 18.

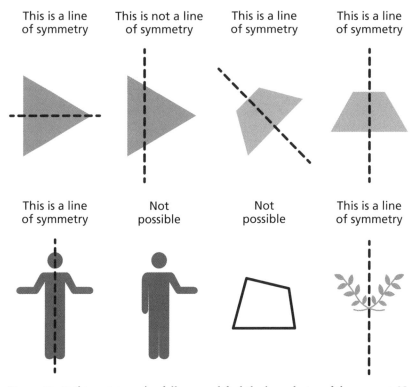

Figure 18: At this point, you've fully exemplified the boundaries of the concept. Now it's time to test

To test whether students understand the concept of symmetry, according to the **testing principle** we should juxtapose new, untaught examples and non-examples in an unpredictable order. The unpredictability is important, as it helps us to rule out that students are just making a 50/50 guess. See Table 11: A good test – either verbal with choral response, or on paper – would look like the one on the left, and not the one on the right because the alternating yes/no is too predictable.

Following the testing principle		Not following the testing principle	
Is this a line of symmetry?	Yes	Is this a line of symmetry?	Yes
Is this a line of symmetry?	No	Is this a line of symmetry?	No
Is this a line of symmetry?	No	Is this a line of symmetry?	Yes
Is this a line of symmetry?	No	Is this a line of symmetry?	No
Is this a line of symmetry?	Yes	Is this a line of symmetry?	Yes
Is this a line of symmetry?	Yes	Is this a line of symmetry?	No

Table 11: Once the boundaries of the concept have been sufficiently exemplified, teachers should present unknown examples in random order to verify that students understand the concept.

✓ Using precise wording, juxtapose minimally different examples to illustrate the boundaries of a concept.

✓ Present a wide range of examples to illustrate sameness.

✓ Test students on unknown instances of the concept to promote generalization.

ERRONEOUS EXAMPLES

One thing I hear a lot in teaching is that we must develop a deeper understanding of the material. What people mean by "deep" is usually unclear and undefined, but we're told to contrast it to "shallow" or "rote learning" – which people can't define either.

Clearly, if a student has retained the information for months after we've presented it to them, we can assume they have learned the material "deeper" than a student who cannot. Additionally, if a student can apply their understanding to a wide range of examples and situations (i.e. as we discussed in the previous section), their learning should be considered deeper than if they can only apply it to a single, narrow instance of the material.

Another way teachers can deepen student understanding is to have students learn from errors (Metcalfe, 2017). **Erroneous examples** are tasks that require the learner to be able to identify errors in *someone else's work* and then fix the errors to produce a correct solution. In the research (e.g. McLaren et al., 2016), erroneous examples tend to employ a fake student, such as Zeke or Miranda, who has a misconception that is typical of students who are learning that particular type of problem. After the students are shown Zeke's or Miranda's improperly solved problem, the teacher prompts them to 1) locate the error, 2) explain the error, and 3) make the appropriate corrections to the problem so that it is solved correctly (Adams et al., 2014).

Another way to think of erroneous examples is that they are simply worked examples with incorrect steps. To illustrate, I'll convert a worked example, where the only task is to learn the steps, into an erroneous example, where the student must use prior knowledge to fix up an incorrect problem (Figure 19).

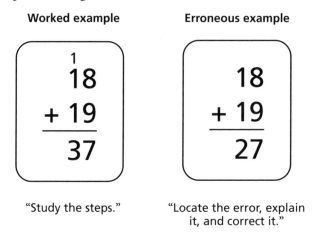

Worked example   **Erroneous example**

"Study the steps."   "Locate the error, explain it, and correct it."

Figure 19: An erroneous example is a worked example with incorrect steps

Providing erroneous examples promotes flexibility of student understanding. Similar to a non-example, they allow us to teach the students *what not to do* when working a problem. Importantly, it probably isn't a good idea to start throwing out erroneous examples before the student can solve similar problems correctly (Barbieri et al., 2023). Launching a unit on writing five paragraph essays by passing out "Nathan's error-filled essay" and then asking students to fix it may sound like a fun, engaging task, but without some knowledge of topic sentences, thesis statements, transition words, and conclusion paragraphs, the students will likely be confused, or even learn bad writing habits from being exposed to the incorrect example.

What clues should we watch for to determine when students are ready to learn from errors? Perhaps counterintuitively, we want to make sure their own performance is relatively *errorless*. I want to be sure that I've thoroughly explained the material multiple times, and used formative assessment to verify that students know the right way to solve the problem. At each point that a student makes an error (e.g. 5 + 3 = 7), I will immediately correct it. The **error correction** procedure I recommend, which I learned in my training on DI, goes something like this:

1. **Correct:** Immediately correct the missed item.

   "Listen: 5 + 3 = 8"

2. **Test:** Ask the students to repeat the correct answer.

   "Your turn, what does 5 + 3 equal?"

3. **Retest:** Give several other items to "flush" the missed item out of working memory, then retest the missed item.

   "What does 5 + 1 equal?" (6!)

   "What does 5 + 2 equal?" (7!)

   "What does 5 + 3 equal?" (8!)

4. **Delayed test:** Retest the item that was missed at various intervals of the day/week.

   "That's right, 5 + 3 = 8. Now I'm going to write 5 + 3 = 8 on a sticky note and test you on it throughout the week so we don't forget!"

   (Adapted from Watkins & Slocum, 2003)

Also, before I give students a task that has them locate and correct errors, I will want to have taught them about the common errors that students at their level tend to make. That way, when the erroneous example is introduced, there will be considerably less guesswork, and less risk of the students internalizing the error as "the correct way." By providing students with erroneous examples, we can help them to avoid common errors in future encounters with the material (McLaren et al., 2016).

- ✓ Show students the correct way to complete the task, and correct errors immediately.
- ✓ Once students are fluent with the material, provide examples of incorrect work so that they can locate and explain the errors.

ANALOGIES

In the neighborhood of providing examples is to use **analogies**, which is when the teacher exemplifies a concept by drawing a comparison between two concepts that seem unrelated at first glance. Similar to using metaphors and similes, the teacher can connect what students already know (e.g. an NFL quarterback) to something that is unknown (e.g. one of history's great wartime generals). The teacher will then home in on the features of the two concepts that they both share: For both quarterbacks and wartime generals, all the moving parts must be considered simultaneously, execution is key, and strategic decisions have consequences. You've already encountered the analogy of the bottleneck and working memory in this very book. The shape of the wine bottle is familiar and concrete to most readers, which helped me to introduce and illustrate the concept of working memory.

Analogies are rarely, if ever, perfect. A game of football is not a matter of life or death, nor does the neck of a wine bottle ever expand (the bottleneck of working memory could be described as *expanding* or disappearing when it encounters topics the learner has already mastered). Despite being imperfect, a good analogy can help students to relate abstract, hard-to-imagine objects or concepts to something the student has seen or knows.

Gray and Holyoak (2021) list several factors that are important to consider when using analogies during teaching:

1. **Capitalize on prior knowledge.**

   It's important to avoid selecting material for comparison that students also don't know much about. Just the other night, I started to tell my daughter that "Learning math is like learning a foreign language" and proceeded to explain the similarities during one of our homework sessions. My daughter nodded respectfully, but as a 4-year-old she knew just as little about what goes into learning a foreign language as she did about what goes into learning math. This is a mistake I've made dozens of times when trying to create an analogy on the fly because young children do not have nearly as many experiences available to them in long-term memory as we adults have. If concept A is equally as unfamiliar to the learner as concept B, the analogy falls apart. For my daughter, comparing the effort of learning math to the effort she invested in learning to ride her tricycle would have worked better.

2. **Highlight shared structure.**

It's important to be explicit about the relations between the two things that are being compared in the analogy. You can't just say the analogy and hope that the inferences are drawn correctly; you also have to explain the analogy. Putting images of the things that are being compared next to each other in a presentation (e.g. an image of a car engine next to that of a mitochondria) helps the learner to draw comparisons more readily. Similar to how an engine powers a car, the mitochondria generate energy for the cell. As the signaling principle suggests in the chapter "Explain with Visuals," teachers should point, underline, circle, color code, and label the parts of the two images that share the features that they want students to compare in the analogy.

3. **Consider cognitive load.**

Introducing an analogy in the learning process can overload working memory, so reducing extraneous load and being explicit early about the relations between the two concepts can help to limit confusion. However, once the teacher has fully explained how A and B are alike, it can be beneficial to get the students to make their own observations, perhaps even generating their own analogies. For example, a teacher could teach the components of a cell by comparing it to a car, and then ask students to make their own analogies using the components of a kitchen (i.e. the nucleus is like a recipe book, the ribosomes are like the cooks, and the endoplasmic reticulum is like the food preparation station). As this book has emphasized many times, it's important to consider students' long-term memories: Having students generate their own analogy may sound creative, but if they don't really have a strong grasp of the concept, they are likely to become overloaded by the task.

✓ Use analogies to compare familiar concepts to more abstract content.

As you think about the principles of example sequencing from this chapter, I encourage you to apply them to something you teach. Most of us teach vocabulary, so pick a word that you are planning to introduce tomorrow and apply these principles. Rather than writing an abstract definition on the board and hoping the students retain it, think about how you will present a range of examples to show what the word means, and what it doesn't mean. Then think about the sort of examples you'll select to test their understanding. By incorporating erroneous examples and analogies into the mix, you'll strengthen students' ability to generalize and apply their understanding to new and unfamiliar contexts.

EXPLAIN WITH STORIES: USE NARRATIVE, EMOTION, AND GESTURES

When I started my career, "engagement" was the be-all and end-all of teaching, and to some tunnel-visioned principals, it remains the only lens they use to observe teaching. As an instructional coach, I've had many teachers come to me hoping I can help them improve their "engagement" so that they might impress the principal on their next evaluation. In fact, this just happened to me the other day.

This was an elementary library teacher, who we'll call Ms. Massoud. When she came to me, it was with tears in her eyes, the kind that you have if you've been crying all night. The principal, she told me, had observed one of her lessons, and had asked the students if they liked learning in her class. Apparently, the students just shrugged or something. The principal then told Ms. Massoud that her lesson wasn't "engaging" enough and she asked that I come to her next lesson and give her some tips.

When I arrived at her lesson, I saw a teacher who welcomed her students to come in, single file, to take a seat on the numbered dots on the carpet. It was calm and orderly. She began her lesson by previewing a new library book, flipping it over to model how a library-goer might investigate if a book is of interest. She then read the back with expression, saying "Oh wow, yes. I think this is it. This is the book I want to read!" She then proceeded to read the book with dramatic voice acting. All eyes were on her, and when at one point she paused for dramatic effect, the room was silent. They were clearly buying what she was selling.

When Ms. Massoud finished the read-aloud, she had the students check out books, and I slid in to have a chat with her.

"What did the principal say about your engagement again?" I asked.

"That I should do more LEGO stuff and scavenger hunts, like the last library teacher always did," she said, her eyes welling up again.

"Oh, for crying out loud. If that guy was a doctor, we'd call him a quack. Did you see the children? Every one of them leaning forward, mouths agape, eyes wide open. You had them hook, line, and sinker. It was freaking beautiful. Keep doing what you're doing, Ms. Massoud. For Pete's sake."

I could go on and on about how engagement has come to mean "entertainment"; how it is used to gaslight and silence teachers; how it is used to blame them for the poor choices that children make; how it is a "theory of everything" among principals who don't know a lick about instruction; but let me get to the point of this chapter. At their core, teachers are not dancing monkeys, stand-up comedians, or circus clowns. However, we can't swing too far in the other direction so as to forget that teaching – and explanation in particular – is a **performance**. And while performing is definitely more on the "art" side of teaching, there are the specific techniques from the scientific literature that teachers should find useful.

STORYTELLING

One of the ways to "engage" students without resorting to LEGO or other gimmicks is to tell stories. The mind seems naturally attuned to stories compared to other modes of explanation. Willingham (2021) puts stories in the category of "psychologically privileged," and suggests teachers use story structure, or **narrativity**, to convey material to students. Even without the benefit of hearing the tone of my voice or the expressions on my face, it's easy to *feel* the difference between an explanation with and without a story structure. Take these two forms of the same text, for example.

1. A young Sudanese boy, aged approximately 10 years, walked for four kilometers to retrieve potable water. Challenges included extreme temperatures and dehydration.

2. In the scorching heat of the Sudanese sun, a young boy, no more than 10 years old, embarked on a daunting quest. His mission was simple yet vital: traverse the arid four kilometer stretch to fetch life-sustaining water. With each step, the relentless sun bore down upon him, threatening dehydration. But within his heart burned a determination fiercer than the sun above.

Stories tune students into the characters and the conflicts that make the material we teach so darn interesting. Life is full of action, drama, and complications. Stories engage the listener with feelings and senses in a way that allows them to experience the events themselves; they paint a vivid picture in the reader's mind. Rather than telling the student, "John was scared," a story might show John's fear by describing his rapid heartbeat, his trembling hands, and his hesitant steps as he enters a dark, abandoned house. This approach helps to create a more immersive and emotionally resonant experience, which makes the content compelling and potentially more memorable.

Willingham (2021) recommends teachers consider the four Cs of storytelling: causality, conflict, complications, and characters. For example, a teacher could use this structure to plan their explanations for the events that led up to the Boston Tea Party: It was a protest against unfair taxation (causality), featuring colonists challenging British authority (conflict), with the act of dumping tea into the harbor symbolizing a bold stand against oppression (complications). Key figures such as Samuel Adams embodied the spirit of resistance (characters), making this event a memorable chapter in the story of America's fight for independence. For me, the classic story structure of exposition, conflict, rising action, climax, falling action, resolution, also does the trick (see Figure 20).

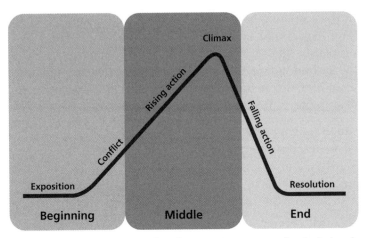

Figure 20: Converting a conventional explanation into a story that includes character and plot development can capture students' attention and imagination

Most storytelling structures employ a "hook" to lure students into the story right away. My go-to when I'm teaching is to start my story off with the words, "Imagine that you ..." *Imagine that you ...* have just stepped out into a bustling market square in ancient Rome. *Imagine that you ...* are a detective in the roaring 1920s, and a high-profile case lands on your desk. This invites the students to step into different worlds to experience the story you are about to tell.

Stories, of course, don't have to be imaginary. Many of the most salient experiences I've provided students were stories that actually happened to me. In talking about how some plants are *invasive species*, I would tell the story of the time when my brother and I were tasked with removing hogweed from my dad's backyard. Hogweed is a sinister-looking plant with long stocks that, we soon found out, were perfect for sword fighting. The thing is, we didn't know that hogweed is also full of toxic chemicals that produce burns and blisters, especially when the skin is subjected to hot sun. Not long after we tired of whacking hogweed juice all over our shirtless chests, we spent the day playing out in the yard in what might have been the hottest day of the summer. For whatever reason, my brother got the burns and blisters, while I only got a small dot on my left arm, which is still visible today. If my dad had read the citation notice the city had sent him more carefully – you know, before he sent his sons out to remove it – he would have known that hogweed aggressively colonizes areas where children play, such as riverbanks and backyards, where it poses a serious health risk. It is an *invasive species*.

✓ Explain with a narrative structure, highlighting the conflict that makes the material so interesting.

EMOTIONAL DESIGN

Many researchers have attempted to describe the role of emotion in the design of instruction (e.g. Immordino-Yang et al., 2018; Mayer & Estrella, 2014). An explanation can elicit emotions such as anxiety, frustration, and boredom, just as it can elicit feelings of joy, inspiration, and curiosity (Tyng et al., 2017). Similar to the clear vs. unclear formats that we discussed from the teacher clarity research, it is easy to see or even "feel" the difference between **emotionally resonant** speech and "dry" speech that seems like it was extracted from an instruction manual. Consider the two ways that a teacher might begin a new novel in Table 12.

Text A	Text B
Today we will be starting *Holes* by Louis Sachar. The text is centered around a juvenile correctional facility called Camp Green Lake and the boys who are serving time there. The book delves into several important themes, which we will explore in detail. Turn to the first page, and let's get started.	Today you begin a journey through the blistering sun of Camp Green Lake – Whew! I'm breaking a sweat just imagining it! – where every shovel of dirt uncovers a piece of history and every character a lesson in friendship, perseverance, and justice. *Holes* is not just a book, my friends. It's an adventure that will dig deep into your heart and stay there long after you turn the last page. Open your books, and get ready to be captivated!

Table 12: Would you want the teacher to launch the book *Holes* with the explanation in Text A or Text B?

There is no contest between these two texts: Text B is clearly better. But what are the specific design features that are embedded in the emotionally resonant text?

Besides highlighting the conflict and using narrativity, the text contains two instances of **personalization**. The first is that the teacher uses the word "you," as in "Today *you* begin a journey through the blistering sun of Camp Green Lake." This, along with "I," "we," and "my friends," puts the student in the middle of the action, and has been found to be superior in research to relying solely on third-person constructions when explaining material (Mayer, 2014). The second instance of personalization is that the teacher uses the self-referencing language of, "Whew! I'm breaking a sweat just imagining it!" The teacher is tapping into the students' emotions by revealing her own feelings about the material to the students.

There are other things that are going on that are harder to convey in a book, but can be described. The teacher in Text B is being **expressive** with her face, which has been shown to have an arousing effect that leads to more learning (Wang, 2022). Expressiveness shows the teacher's personal investment in what the students are doing, which has a way of rubbing off on the learner. Also present, but hidden from us in the text on the right, is the use of "motivational prosody" (Paulmann & Weinstein, 2023), or an inviting and supportive **tone of voice**. Harsh, controlling, negative, weak, strained, and otherwise unpleasant tones of voice have been shown to be associated with lower satisfaction and retention of material, but more research is needed in classroom settings. In multimedia research, human voices have been shown to increase learning compared to when the same information is presented by a robotic voice (Mayer, 2017).

Finally, we should imagine that the texts differ to the extent that the two teachers use **eye contact** with students. The teacher on the right side intentionally, almost exaggeratedly, switches gaze from one student to the next in an effort to bring everyone into the fold. Research supports this technique: eye contact helps to regulate students' attention toward the speaker's communication goals (Hietanen, 2018), and can be used "to read the room." Is my audience with me, or not?

✓ Tap into students' emotions by revealing your own feelings about the material.

✓ Use eye contact, facial expressions, and an emotionally resonant tone of voice when explaining.

GESTURES

It's weird sometimes what helps make stuff you learned "stick" so that it remains with you later in life. That is the point of this book, after all. I remember when my Seventh grade teacher gave us a text describing the three fundamental ways a spaceship maneuvers in space: Pitch, Yaw, and Roll.

- **Pitch:** This refers to the rotation of a spacecraft around its lateral axis. When a spaceship pitches, its nose either tilts upward or downward, relative to its direction of travel.

- **Yaw:** This involves the rotation of a spacecraft around its vertical axis. When a spaceship yaws, it changes its orientation horizontally.

- **Roll:** Rolling is the rotation of a spacecraft around its longitudinal axis. When a spaceship rolls, it changes its orientation side to side.

But, like so many abstract things, the teacher needed a way to explain the information so it was more concrete. So, she used gestures. Roll was easy: she had us put our hands out, extended, and twist, like rolling a toy car along its length.

For Pitch, she nodded her head (just as a baseball pitcher does when saying "yes" to accept a pitch) and had us pitch an invisible ball (awkwardly) in the same motion. For Yaw, she did a goofy retro dance move, gesturing side to side, saying "Yaw, man." It was so fun to play along, her orchestrating, us copying the gestures and pairing them with the new vocabulary, and here I am, remembering it vividly, decades later.

But gestures are more than for fun or memorizing. Gestures are a natural, fundamental part of speech, what cognitive scientists call "co-speech" (Clough & Duff, 2020). Babies use gestures before they can speak, and blind children who have never themselves seen gestures, will gesture while speaking (Roth, 2001).

Gestures are particularly well suited for communicating visuo-spatial information compared to speech alone, similar to how viewing images paired with speech helps students to integrate information from the two "codes" into a single mental representation. This is related to theories of **embodiment** and **social agency**: gestures guide cognitive processing and foster a sense of social partnership (Mayer et al., 2020).

If gestures help students learn but are also something everyone does naturally, are there things teachers can do to maximize the efficacy of their gestures to improve explanations?

For a start, it is important for the teacher to be visible while explaining so that the students can see both their gestures and facial expressions. *Teach from the front, people!* As you command the room from up there, use your body to gain attention. Put your hand in the air to complement your auditory signal, and insist on all eyes on you, the speaker. Then, as you start your explanation, use your hands and arms to envelop attention, signaling to the board, pointing to students' notebooks when it is time to use them, moving closer to students who need direct supervision, and stepping away from the student who is speaking, to signal to the rest of the students that they must pay attention (Boxer, 2024). Lastly, teachers can plan out representational gestures, just as my teacher did with the Pitch, Yaw, and Roll example. Getting students to mimic the gestures we use and trace the information we put in front of them (Du & Zhang, 2019) can improve memory.

✓ Use gestures to represent material and guide cognitive processing.

EXPLAIN AND RELEASE: GRADUALLY FADE GUIDANCE

There are times when it is essential to explain the material to students, but eventually, explanations are no longer necessary. In this chapter, we will explore the pivotal role that explanations play in initial instruction, and their diminishing effectiveness as students master the material. As we'll see shortly, the volume or "dosage" of explanations that students receive is largely determined by ongoing changes in their **expertise**.

NOVICES VS. EXPERTS

When students have low prior knowledge about a given topic, whether it's how to solve the quadratic equation or blend the sounds /s/ and /p/ at the beginning of the word "spell," they are considered **novices**. They are beginners who, for the moment, are new and unpracticed in *the specific area* that is being taught.

Novice   Expert

Figure 21: The expert–novice continuum describes the path from being new to the material to knowing it inside and out

But novices do not stay total novices for very long. When explanations are effective, the students will begin to internalize these communications. Material that was once foreign, and perhaps even intimidating, will gradually become intuitive and second nature. At some point, the students will become so proficient with the material that we can no longer consider them novices, or even "intermediates," with the material. We can call them **experts**, in the sense that they've reached such a high level of mastery in the topic at hand (i.e. the quadratic equation or /s/ and /p/ blends) that completing tasks on that topic is fluent and effortless. Ultimately, the goal of the teacher is to ensure that every single student, regardless of how far behind they might have started, achieves the status of expert in each area of the curriculum that they've been entrusted to teach them.

It is more fruitful to think of expert–novice differences as existing on a continuum (Figure 21) rather than as a binary, one-or-the-other situation. As we accumulate and organize more knowledge about a subject, we gradually move along this continuum toward expertise. There isn't a specific point where we suddenly switch from novice to expert; instead, it's a gradual progression. We should also view expert–novice differences as being **domain-specific**. Just because a student has mastered the 44 phonemes of phonics instruction, for example, doesn't mean that they have achieved expertise in counting, or anything else for that matter.

Recognizing that expertise exists on a continuum and is domain-specific allows us to tailor our teaching approaches based on learners' existing knowledge. Contrary to what many of us were told in teacher school, it is a bad idea to expect novices to discover the material on their own. They need the teacher to structure the learning with explanations, examples, and demonstrations if they are to acquire new and unfamiliar information. However, once students begin to demonstrate mastery in a topic, the teacher should begin the process of *reducing* the amount of direct instructional guidance they provide (Kalyuga & Sweller, 2018). Teachers must continuously adapt their methods to changes in expertise, so that by the end of the continuum the methods that were better suited for novices are eventually replaced with methods suited for experts. In cognitive load theory, this is known as the **expertise reversal effect**.

In both my own teaching and in my work as an instructional coach, I've experienced countless lessons in which the challenge of tasks and the scaffolding was poorly calibrated. With different cohorts of students having different levels of prior knowledge, it is easy to make incorrect assumptions about how fast or slow to fade supports. With the pressure of covering the curriculum looming over our heads, the process of "gradually releasing" students into independent practice can become rushed, haphazard, or nonexistent. Consider each of the following (real) examples in which the students were, to put it bluntly, "thrown into the deep end" during a lesson before they had acquired the skills they needed to be successful:

1. Ms. Clarke begins an elementary science lesson by passing out hands-on materials for a unit on states of matter. The students are noticeably excited, and there are a few instances when Ms. Clarke has to reprimand students for touching the materials early. Once the activity begins, Ms. Clarke circulates the room to give each table pointers and hints. The problem is, the students are not really listening to her pointers and hints due to the distracting presence of the materials and the noise level in the room. Ms. Clarke also has a hard time getting around to everyone because there are so many questions about what to do and how to use the materials. The result is that several students have folded their arms in frustration, some are building towers with the materials, one group is busily mopping up a large water spill, and one student has been put in "time out." Most alarmingly, very few of the students are observed applying or discussing scientific knowledge of states of matter during the activity.

2. Mr. Nelson takes pride in teaching world history through role play, encouraging students to engage in dramatic debates about historical events. Today, the building's instructional coach has been invited to observe the launch of a role play about the encounters between the Spanish conquistadors and the Aztecs. The coach notes that it starts off strong, but that it begins to fall apart once the students have used up the information contained in their role-play guides. One by one, students begin to tune out of the discussion, and soon the role play is reduced to a single conversation between just two or three students. When one student complains, "Mr. Nelson, this is boring!" Mr. Nelson launches into a lecture about how he is trying to teach critical thinking, and how the system has ruined students' capacity to think for themselves. "Fine," he relents. "If you want me to do all the talking, I'll teach at the board." Not only is the rest of the lesson unnecessarily tense, but the observing coach notes several crucial pieces of historical information from Mr. Nelson's ensuing presentation that the students could have used in their role play had Mr. Nelson taught it to them in advance.

3. Ms. LoFranco places five posters around the room, each with a different word problem on them. She gives each student a marker, and delivers clear instructions about class expectations during the activity. Before setting the students loose, she warns the class that the word problems were chosen because they contain math skills that she hasn't covered yet. "It is important that we engage in a bit of productive struggle during this activity. It is not about getting the right answer, but about the process of engaging our thinking muscles." While the class maintains focus and good behavior throughout the poster activity, the instructional coach notes a few things. First, it is the students who already know the math that are making the majority of the contributions. The rest of the students, including the students with special education needs, are either staring blankly at the posters, copying from the more advanced students, or engaging in guesswork. Second, the coach notices that Ms. LoFranco intentionally avoids providing models and examples throughout the activity, even when the students request them. Each time a student hits a roadblock, Ms. LoFranco says things like, "I think you can figure this out on your own" or "Have you fully analyzed the problem?"

While the ages of the students and the subject matter in these three lessons differed, there was an important commonality that they all shared: the teachers didn't explain the material upfront so that the students could engage successfully in the planned activity. The students were at serious risk of cognitive overload, which can express itself in a variety of ways. Some students may decide to simply give up, while others will suddenly find the desire to misbehave (better to look like you don't care than to look stupid, after all). Some of the more persistent students may just randomly guess, or copy from others, while others may develop anxious feelings or a negative self-concept around the topic (Mesghina et al., 2023). What we can be reasonably sure of is that the students probably won't learn much from persisting through tasks that require them to discover solutions that could easily be explained to them (Mayer, 2004; Sweller, 2021).

✓ Explain the material early and often during the initial stages of skill acquisition.

✓ Slowly reduce the amount of explanation as students gain competence with the material.

Fortunately for us, the literature offers many techniques to gradually fade guidance. These come from research into cognitive load theory, the instructional design principles of DI, and research into the most effective teachers (Rosenshine, 2012).

TUTORIAL ON FADING GUIDANCE

A common misconception about cognitive load theory is that it's about making learning as easy as possible, when in fact it's about *managing* working memory load so that it is neither too high nor too low. Explaining the material, as the worked example effect shows, is an effective way to take the burden off the novice learner as they're learning something new. Once novice students have benefited from some initial models and examples, working the material in full for them becomes counterproductive, as the students will possess sufficient knowledge and skills in long-term memory to be able to complete portions of the material on their own (see Figure 22).

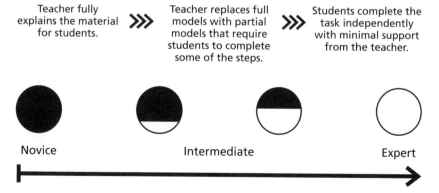

Figure 22: The teacher should gradually replace scaffolds (the black) with student practice opportunities (the white) as their knowledge and skill increases

Let's follow the teacher below as she starts her guidance fading sequence with full modeling (I do), proceeds to partial modeling (We do), and ends with students completing the entire task on their own (You do).

With all eyes on her to start the lesson, the teacher uncaps her marker, and clearly and succinctly demonstrates how to add fractions with unlike denominators (Figure 23). While we'll be analyzing a math worked example in this tutorial, we could just as easily be looking at a diagram showing a science process (i.e. the water cycle), or a teacher's explanation of a tricky segment of text (i.e. a Shakespearean sonnet).

Worked example

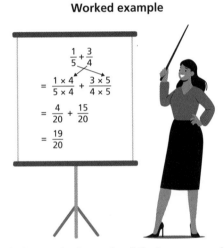

Figure 23: In this worked example, the teacher fully demonstrates how to add fractions, starting with finding a common denominator, and ending with adding like fractions to produce the correct answer, 19/20

After her presentation of the worked example, the teacher moves to the second phase of her guidance fading: the use of a **completion problem** or a "partial example" rather than another worked example (Figure 24). She says, "I am now going to work out another problem with slightly different numbers, but this time you will have to complete the final step of the problem on your mini whiteboards." A "3, 2, 1 … show me" reveals that the students have correctly answered the final solution step (i.e. the question mark).

Completion problem 1 – Omit final step

Figure 24: Completion problem 1 is a teacher-worked problem, except the final step is left blank for students to solve

Offering a completion problem *after* a worked example solves a couple of issues that are common in classroom learning. First, it keeps the cognitive load of the task at an optimal level by gradually reducing guidance. Rather than throwing students in the "deep end" by giving them a full problem to solve, the teacher requires them to work out one, and only one, step on their own. From a motivational perspective, informing students that they must complete the final step of the problem on their mini whiteboards tends to encourage them to pay close attention to the teacher's modeling so that they may answer their part correctly.

After the first completion problem, the teacher proceeds to completion problem 2. This time, two steps are omitted, as shown in Figure 25.

Completion problem 2 – Omit final two steps

Figure 25: Completion problem 2 is a teacher-worked problem, except the teacher now has students solve the final two steps

The teacher always chooses slightly different numbers to ensure that the students are applying the strategy rather than copying, and then begins to fade her example so that the students are completing the final three steps (Figure 26).

Completion problem 3 – Omit steps until independent problem solving achieved

Figure 26: Completion problem 3 has the teacher only solving the first step, with the students solving the rest of the problem

By the end, the students are completing all of the steps on their own without any steps being worked by the teacher. Figure 27 shows the full transition between the teacher fully explaining the material and students completing the task on their own.

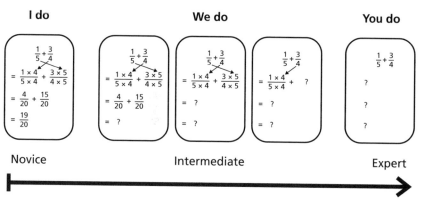

Figure 27: The gradual release model, aka the guidance fading effect and I do, We do, You do

In my experience observing lessons, I often see only the "I do" and "You do" segments of Figure 27. Perhaps the teacher briefly explains the material at the board before passing out an assignment with dozens of similar problems. What's missing is the "We do" in the middle that eases students into being able to complete the task independently. Teachers should engage students in guided practice, where they work through the problems together, ask questions, and provide corrective feedback. This crucial step of the gradual release model helps to solidify understanding and build confidence before students are asked to tackle the material on their own.

✓ Gradually omit steps in explanations so that the responsibility of completing the material increasingly rests with the students.

✓ Use an "I do, We do, You do" sequence to explain material to students.

ADDITIONAL GUIDANCE FADING CALIBRATIONS

As we've just seen, great explainers start with an emphasis on the teacher's role as the source of information and move to an emphasis on the learner as the source of information. To close out this chapter, we will look at additional techniques from DI that are critical to making the gradual release truly, well, gradual.

GO FROM OUT LOUD TO IN THEIR HEAD

As I've stressed throughout this book, effective explanations are interactive, and this is particularly true at the beginning of the sequence when students are just learning the material. After a teacher explains the material to students, she will want to hear them say it back *aloud* to check that students were listening. She will need to lean heavily on choral response so that all students revoice the material at the same time, and she will want to use cold calling to collect individual responses. Turn and talks and mini whiteboards play a role here, too.

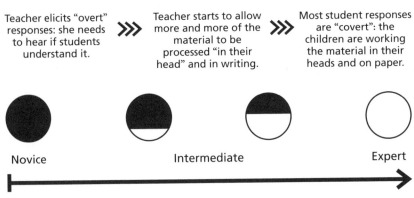

Figure 28: The overt-to-covert sequence of guidance fading

Once the students have demonstrated their new knowledge out loud, the teacher will shift to allowing students to work on the material on their own, covertly. Here's an example. The teacher says aloud five math facts, $1 + 5 = 6$, $2 + 5 = 7$, $3 + 5 = 8$, $4 + 5 = 9$ and $5 + 5 = 10$, and has students practice saying the facts aloud with choral response. He tests them with mini whiteboards. Once he is certain that students can say each of these facts aloud without a problem, correcting each fact until firm, he has students work on a worksheet that contains each of these facts in random order. Of course, he circulates and corrects for errors here too, but by employing the overt-to-covert sequence, he can be sure that virtually all students will be successful on their more "private" independent task.

GO FROM SIMPLE TO COMPLEX

When students are novices, each new *element* we present to them is an item that must be processed in limited working memory. We can call a task "simple" if it contains relatively few of these elements to grapple with. A "complex" task, on the other hand, contains a high number of elements for the novice to process. Complexity is also largely the function of how many items must be processed simultaneously. Memorizing a list of words may contain a lot of items, but the task is relatively low in complexity because each can be processed individually. On the other hand, asking a kindergartener who hasn't fully mastered the phonetic code to read a Fifth grade text is a task that is extremely high in **element interactivity** (Chen et al., 2018). The task requires students to do a lot of hard things at the same time, including blending sounds together, attending to unfamiliar vocabulary, deciphering the complexities of the plot, and so on. A key reason that explicit phonics instruction is so effective is that it isolates phonemes, allowing beginning readers to focus solely on learning them without the additional demands of reading that are found in whole texts.

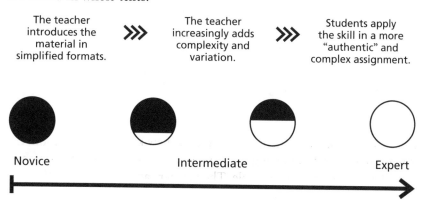

Figure 29: Teachers can avoid overloading their students by teaching the components of a complex task in isolation and then gradually recombining them

Teachers must build up to complex assignments by teaching parts of the whole task in isolation. In cognitive load theory, this is called the **isolated elements effect** (Pollock et al., 2002). Once students have undergone a bit of modeling and part-task practice of prerequisite skills, the teacher should slowly combine the elements together. The reason this won't overload students is that they have become so fluent in each of the isolated elements through part-task practice that these no longer constitute multiple interacting elements, but can be retrieved from long-term memory with minimal impact on working memory. By the end of the sequence, the students should be working on the "complex" assignment, but thanks to the foundation that was laid beforehand, the cognitive load it imposes will have been brought down to manageable levels.

GO FROM MASSED PRACTICE TO SPACED PRACTICE

We have come to the end, folks, and what a ride it has been. Picture yourself having introduced the material with crystal clarity and stunning visuals. You've broken down the material into its components, and you've built it back up so that students can do the composite task independently. That was all **massed practice** involving continuous, concentrated teaching of a specific skill over a short period of time. Now it is time to fade the material out so that students can work on other things (Figure 30).

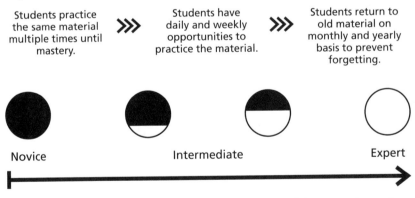

Figure 30: At first, students will need multiple repetitions of the material in order to learn it, but as the year goes on these can become less and less frequent

We hardly want the students to forget what we've taught them, so we mix in some of the most important bits of the material throughout the year.

We embed it in our "Do Nows" and class discussions. Perhaps we have at least one test item from past units appear in all future tests. Like artists, we weave old knowledge into future learning, having students connect what we taught them earlier in the year with new information from the current unit. All of this **spaced practice** is in service of halting that pesky forgetting curve, but also to give students that satisfaction of, "Hey, I'm powerful. I know things." As teachers, our greatest gift to our students is the confidence to interact with the world as competent, flexible, critical thinkers. And it all started with an explanation.

✓ Break complex material down into part-tasks and gradually build up to whole tasks.

✓ Gradually shift from overt to covert responses, and massed practice to spaced practice.

CONCLUSION

As a new teacher, I wanted to please others and was worried about the optics of being seen as the expert explaining at the front of the room. I was under the impression that teacher talk was simply ineffective because, well, lots of people who should have known better told me so. Ultimately, I may have embraced the guide-on-the-side mentality because it reflected my overly idealistic view of teaching. Some small part of me still wishes that students learned best when given the chance to discover the material on their own.

These days, I am deeply concerned about the so-called "low" and "at-risk" students in our schools who have been let down by a system that favors minimally guided approaches over evidence and common sense. These students had teachers who surrounded them with books instead of teaching them phonics, and with tubs of math games instead of teaching them their math facts. Many of these students end up requiring intensive interventions to help them catch up, and the "cure" is almost always for the interventionist to teach more explicitly than the student can expect in a general education setting. One has to wonder why that wasn't prescribed in the first place. If these students are lucky, they will be assigned a teacher who explains things exceptionally well; a teacher who has mastered the art of "breaking it down" so that learning feels easy. Then, for a fleeting moment each day, they can forget their challenges – challenges that were largely preventable – and experience what it feels like to "be smart." I'm not old enough or jaded enough to give up on these kids.

What do I hope you got out of this book? I hope you saw that while explanation is grounded in scientific principles and encompasses various techniques, doing it well is not the privilege of those who were "born" doing it well but something that can be designed and practiced. And I hope you go into your classroom tomorrow with the knowledge that, no matter how small we are in numbers, there are others out there who are working every day to master this humble art, even if it isn't the most trendy or sexy way to teach. We'll keep chugging on to ensure that every student gets the world-class education they deserve. Finally, I hope that, the next time you find yourself "facilitating" a class of students who have "productively struggled" far past their limits, and the devil on your shoulder keeps whispering, "They'll only learn it if they discover it for themselves," you will give the devil a flick and just freaking tell them.

REFERENCES

Adams, D. M., McLaren, B. M., Durkin, K., Mayer, R. E., Rittle-Johnson, B., Isotani, S., & Van Velsen, M. (2014). Using Erroneous Examples to Improve Mathematics Learning with a Web-Based Tutoring System. *Computers in Human Behavior*, 36, 401–11. https://doi.org/10.1016/j.chb.2014.03.053

Albers, F., Trypke, M., Stebner, F., Wirth, J., & Plass, J. L. (2023). Different Types of Redundancy and Their Effect on Learning and Cognitive Load. *British Journal of Educational Psychology*. https://doi.org/10.1111/bjep.12592

Archer, A., & Hughes, C. (2011). Exploring the Foundations of Explicit Instruction. In *Explicit Instruction: Effective and Efficient Teaching* (pp. 1–22). Guilford Press.

Barbieri, C. A., Miller-Cotto, D., Clerjuste, S. N., & Chawla, K. (2023). A Meta-Analysis of the Worked Examples Effect on Mathematics Performance. *Educational Psychology Review*, 35(1). https://doi.org/10.1007/s10648-023-09745-1

Bisra, K., Liu, Q., Nesbit, J. C., Salimi, F., & Winne, P. H. (2018). Inducing Self-Explanation: A Meta-Analysis. *Educational Psychology Review*, 30(3), 703–25. https://doi.org/10.1007/s10648-018-9434-x

Boxer, A. (2024). Step Away from the Speaker: MCA1. *A Chemical Orthodoxy* (January 18). https://achemicalorthodoxy.co.uk/2024/01/18/step-away-from-the-speaker-mca1/

Bronzaft, A. L., & McCarthy, D. P. (1975). The Effect of Elevated Train Noise on Reading Ability. *Environment and Behavior*, 7(4), 517-28. https://doi.org/10.1177/001391657500700406

Brophy, J. (1986). Classroom Management Techniques. *Education and Urban Society*, 18(2), 182–94. https://doi.org/10.1177/0013124586018002005

Castro-Alonso, J.C. & Sweller, J. (2020) The Modality Effect of Cognitive Load Theory. In: Karwowski, W., Ahram, T., & Nazir, S. (eds) *Advances in Human Factors in Training, Education, and Learning Sciences.*

AHFE 2019. Advances in Intelligent Systems and Computing, vol 963. Springer, Cham. https://doi.org/10.1007/978-3-030-20135-7_7

Caviglioli, O. (2019). *Dual Coding With Teachers*. John Catt Educational.

Chen, O., Castro-Alonso, J. C., Paas, F., & Sweller, J. (2018). Undesirable Difficulty Effects in the Learning of High-Element Interactivity Materials. *Frontiers in Psychology, 9* (August). https://doi.org/10.3389/fpsyg.2018.01483

Caviola, S., Visentin, C., Borella, E., Mammarella, I., & Prodi, N. (2021). Out of the Noise: Effects of Sound Environment on Maths Performance in Middle-School Students. *Journal of Environmental Psychology, 73*. https://doi.org/10.1016/j.jenvp.2021.101552

Christakou, A., Vasileiadis, G., & Kapreli, E. (2019). Motor Imagery as a Method of Maintaining Performance in Pianists During Forced Non-Practice: A Single Case Study. *Physiotherapy Theory and Practice, 37*(4), 540–48. https://doi.org/10.1080/09593985.2019.1636917

Christodoulou, D. (2014). Minding the Knowledge Gap. *American Educator* (Spring), 27–33.

Clinton, V., Alibali, M. W., & Nathan, M. J. (2016). Learning about Posterior Probability: Do Diagrams and Elaborative Interrogation Help? *Journal of Experimental Education, 84*(3), 579–99. https://doi.org/10.1080/00220973.2015.1048847

Clough, S., & Duff, M. C. (2020). The Role of Gesture in Communication and Cognition: Implications for Understanding and Treating Neurogenic Communication Disorders. *Frontiers in Human Neuroscience, 14*. https://doi.org/10.3389/fnhum.2020.00323

Cowan, N. (2001). The Magical Number 4 in Short-Term Memory: A Reconsideration of Mental Storage Capacity. *Behavioral and Brain Sciences, 24*(1), 87–114. https://doi.org/10.1017/S0140525X01003922

Dallimore, E. J., Hertenstein, J. H., & Platt, M. B. (2013). Impact of Cold-Calling on Student Voluntary Participation. *Journal of Management Education, 37*(3), 305–41. https://doi.org/10.1177/1052562912446067

Dallimore, E. J., Hertenstein, J. H., & Platt, M. B. (2019). Leveling the Playing Field: How Cold-Calling Affects Class Discussion Gender Equity.

Journal of Education and Learning, 8(2), 14. https://doi.org/10.5539/jel. v8n2p14

Daniyal, M., Javaid, S. F., Hassan, A., & Khan, M. A. B. (2022). The Relationship between Cellphone Usage on the Physical and Mental Wellbeing of University Students: A Cross-Sectional Study. *International Journal of Environmental Research and Public Health*, 19(15). https://doi. org/10.3390/ijerph19159352

Du, X., & Zhang, Q. (2019). Tracing Worked Examples: Effects on Learning in Geometry. *Educational Psychology*, 39(2), 169–87. https://doi. org/10.1080/01443410.2018.1536256

Engelmann, S., & Carnine, D. (2016). *Theory of Instruction: Principles and Applications*. NIFDI Press.

Fiorella, L., & Mayer, R. E. (2016). Eight Ways to Promote Generative Learning. *Educational Psychology Review*, 28(4), 717–41. https://doi. org/10.1007/s10648-015-9348-9

Fisher, A. V., Godwin, K. E., & Seltman, H. (2014). Visual Environment, Attention Allocation, and Learning in Young Children: When Too Much of a Good Thing May Be Bad. *Psychological Science*, 25(7), 1362–70. https://doi.org/10.1177/0956797614533801

Forrin, N. D., Huynh, A. C., Smith, A. C., Cyr, E. N., McLean, D. B., Siklos-Whillans, J., Risko, E. F., Smilek, D., & MacLeod, C. M. (2021). Attention Spreads Between Students in a Learning Environment. *Journal of Experimental Psychology: Applied*, 27(2), 276–91. https://doi. org/10.1037/xap0000341

Godwin, K. E., Leroux, A. J., Seltman, H., Scupelli, P., & Fisher, A. V. (2022). Effect of Repeated Exposure to the Visual Environment on Young Children's Attention. *Cognitive Science*, 46(2). https://doi.org/10.1111/ cogs.13093

Gray, M. E., & Holyoak, K. J. (2021). Teaching by Analogy: From Theory to Practice. *Mind, Brain, and Education*, 15(3), 250–63. https://doi. org/10.1111/mbe.12288

Heward, W. L., & Wood, C. L. (2015). *Improving Educational Outcomes in America: Can a Low-Tech, Generic Teaching Practice Make a Difference? [Paper presentation]*. Wing Institute's Eighth Annual

Summit on Evidence-Based Education. www.winginstitute.org/uploads/docs/2013WingSummitWH.pdf

Hietanen, J. K. (2018). Affective Eye Contact: An Integrative Review. *Frontiers in Psychology*, 9. https://doi.org/10.3389/fpsyg.2018.01587

Hughes, C. A., Riccomini, P. J., & Morris, J. R. (2019). Use Explicit Instruction. *High Leverage Practices for Inclusive Classrooms* (November), 215–36. https://doi.org/10.4324/9781315176093-20

Immordino-Yang, M. H., Darling-Hammond, L., & Krone, C. (2018). The Brain Basis for Integrated Social, Emotional, and Academic Development: How Emotions and Social Relationships Drive Learning. *National Commission on Social, Emotional and Academic Development*, 20.

Kalyuga, S., & Sweller, J. (2018). Cognitive Load and Expertise Reversal. In K. A. Ericsson, R. R. Hoffman, & A. Kozbelt (eds.), *The Cambridge Handbook of Expertise and Expert Performance* (pp. 793–811). Cambridge University Press. https://doi.org/10.1017/9781316480748.040

Kern, L., & Clemens, N. H. (2007). Antecedent Strategies to Promote Appropriate Classroom Behavior. *Psychology in the Schools*, 44(1), 65–75. https://doi.org/10.1002/pits.20206

Kirschner, P. A., Sweller, J., & Clark, R. E. (2006). Why Minimal Guidance During Instruction Does Not Work: An Analysis of the Failure of Constructivist, Discovery, Problem-Based, Experiential, and Inquiry-Based Teaching. *Educational Psychologist*, 41(2), 75–86. https://doi.org/10.1207/s15326985ep4102_1

Lin, L., & Atkinson, R. K. (2013). Enhancing Learning from Different Visualizations by Self-Explanation Prompts. *Journal of Educational Computing Research*, 49(1), 83–110. https://doi.org/10.2190/EC.49.1.d

Ling Lo, M. (2012). *Variation Theory and the Improvement of Teaching and Learning*. Gothenburg: Acta Universitatis Gothoburgensis.

Ling Lo, M., & Marton, F. (2011). Towards a Science of the Art of Teaching. *International Journal for Lesson and Learning Studies*, 1(1), 7–22. https://doi.org/10.1108/20468251211179678

MacSuga-Gage, A. S., & Gage, N. A. (2015). Student-Level Effects of Increased Teacher-Directed Opportunities to Respond. *Journal of*

Behavioral Education, 24(3), 273–88. https://doi.org/10.1007/s10864-015-9223-2

Massonnié, J., Frasseto, P., Mareschal, D., & Kirkham, N. Z. (2022). Learning in Noisy Classrooms: Children's Reports of Annoyance and Distraction from Noise Are Associated with Individual Differences in Mind-Wandering and Switching Skills. *Environment and Behavior, 54*(1), 58-88. https://doi.org/10.1177/0013916520950277

Mayer, R. E. (2004). Should There Be a Three-Strikes Rule Against Pure Discovery Learning? *American Psychologist, 59*(1), 14–19. https://doi.org/10.1037/0003-066x.59.1.14

Mayer, R. E. (2014). *The Cambridge Handbook of Multimedia Learning.* Cambridge University Press.

Mayer, R. E. (2017). Using Multimedia for E-Learning. *Journal of Computer Assisted Learning, 33*(5), 403–23. https://doi.org/10.1111/jcal.12197

Mayer, R. E., & Estrella, G. (2014). Benefits of Emotional Design in Multimedia Instruction. *Learning and Instruction, 33*, 12–18. https://doi.org/10.1016/j.learninstruc.2014.02.004

Mayer, R. E., Fiorella, L., & Stull, A. (2020). Five Ways to Increase the Effectiveness of Instructional Video. *Educational Technology Research and Development, 68*(3), 837–52. https://doi.org/10.1007/s11423-020-09749-6

Mayer, R. E., Heiser, J., & Lonn, S. (2001). Cognitive Constraints on Multimedia Learning: When Presenting More Material Results in Less Understanding. *Journal of Educational Psychology, 93*(1), 187–98. https://doi.org/10.1037/0022-0663.93.1.187

McLaren, B. M., Van Gog, T., Ganoe, C., Karabinos, M., & Yaron, D. (2016). The Efficiency of Worked Examples Compared to Erroneous Examples, Tutored Problem Solving, and Problem Solving in Computer-Based Learning Environments. *Computers in Human Behavior, 55*, 87–99. https://doi.org/10.1016/j.chb.2015.08.038

Mesghina, A., Vollman, E., Trezise, K., & Richland, L. E. (2023). Worked Examples Moderate the Effect of Math Learning Anxiety on Children's Math Learning and Engagement during the COVID-19 Pandemic.

Journal of Educational Psychology, *116*(2), 173–94. https://doi.org/10.1037/edu0000795

Metcalfe, J. (2017). Learning from Errors. *Annual Review of Psychology*, *68*(1), 465–89. https://doi.org/10.1146/annurev-psych-010416-044022

Miller, G. A. (1956). The Magical Number Seven, Plus or Minus Two: Some Limits on Our Capacity for Processing Information. *Psychological Review*, *63*(2), 81–97. https://doi.org/10.1037/h0043158

NAEP. (2023). *The Nation's Report Card*. https://nces.ed.gov/nationsreportcard/

OECD. (2023). *PISA 2022 Results (Volume II): Learning During – and From – Disruption*. OECD Publishing, Paris. https://doi.org/10.1787/a97db61c-en

Oksa, A., Kalyuga, S., & Chandler, P. (2010). Expertise Reversal Effect in Using Explanatory Notes for Readers of Shakespearean Text. *Instructional Science*, *38*(3), 217–36.

Paas, F. & van Merriënboer, J.J.G. (2020). Cognitive-load theory: Methods to manage working memory load in the learning of complex tasks. *Current Directions in Psychological Science*, *29*(4), 394–98. https://doi.org/10.1177/0963721420922183

Paulmann, S., & Weinstein, N. (2023). Teachers' Motivational Prosody: A Pre-Registered Experimental Test of Children's Reactions to Tone of Voice Used by Teachers. *British Journal of Educational Psychology*, *93*(2), 437–52. https://doi.org/10.1111/bjep.12567

Perham, N., & Currie, H. (2014). Does Listening to Preferred Music Improve Reading Comprehension Performance? *Applied Cognitive Psychology*, *28*(2), 279–84. https://doi.org/10.1002/acp.2994

Pink, A., & Newton, P. M. (2020). Decorative Animations Impair Recall and Are a Source of Extraneous Cognitive Load. *Advances in Physiology Education*, *44*(3), 376–82. https://doi.org/10.1152/advan.00102.2019

Pollock, E., Chandler, P., & Sweller, J. (2002). Assimilating Complex Information. *Learning and Instruction*, *12*(1), 61–86. https://doi.org/10.1016/S0959-4752(01)00016-0

Pomerance, L., Greenberg, J., Walsh, K., Canada, T., Crawford-Gleeson, M., Khalid, M., Klauda, S., Dunlosky, J., Winn, J. L., Botman, S., Boyd, S., Connolly, J., Finn, C. E., Fishman, I., Watson Garlett, M., Johnson, H. L., & Lasley, T. (2016). *Learning About Learning*. https://www.nctq. org/publications/Learning-About-Learning:-What-Every-New-Teacher-Needs-to-Know

Rance, G., Dowell, R. C., & Tomlin, D. (2023). The Effect of Classroom Environment on Literacy Development. *NPJ Science of Learning, 8*(1). https://doi.org/10.1038/s41539-023-00157-y

Renkl, A. (2002). Worked-Out Examples: Instructional Explanations Support Learning by Self-Explanations. *Learning and Instruction, 12*(5), 529–56. https://doi.org/10.1016/S0959-4752(01)00030-5

Rosenshine, B. (2012). Principles of Instruction: Research-Based Strategies that all Teachers Should Know. *American Educator* (Spring), 12–20.

Roth, W. M. (2001). Gestures: Their Role in Teaching and Learning. *Review of Educational Research, 71*(3), 365–92. https://doi. org/10.3102/00346543071003365

Serki, N., & Bolkan, S. (2023). The Effect of Clarity on Learning: Impacting Motivation Through Cognitive Load. *Communication Education*, 1–17. https://doi.org/10.1080/03634523.2023.2250883

Smith, A. M., Floerke, V. A., & Thomas, A. K. (2016). Retrieval Practice Protects Memory Against Acute Stress. *Science, 354*(6315), 1046–8. https://doi.org/10.1126/science.aah5067

Smith, J. L. M., Sáez, L., & Doabler, C. T. (2016). Using Explicit and Systematic Instruction to Support Working Memory. *Teaching Exceptional Children, 48*(6), 275–81. https://doi.org/10.1177/0040059916650633

Smith, L. R., & Cotten, M. L. (1980). Effect of Lesson Vagueness and Discontinuity on Student Achievement and Attitudes. *Journal of Educational Psychology, 72*(5), 670–5. https://doi.org/10.1037/0022-0663.72.5.670

Smith, L. R., & Land, M. L. (1981). Low-Inference Verbal Behaviors Related to Teacher Clarity. *Journal of Classroom Interaction, 17*(1), 37–42. www.jstor.org/stable/43997776

Stahl, R. J. (1994). Using "Think-Time" and "Wait-Time" Skillfully in the Classroom. *Eric Digest, ED370885*, 1–6. https://files.eric.ed.gov/fulltext/ED370885.pdf

Stewart, A. A., & Swanson, E. (2019). *Turn and Talk: An Evidence-Based Practice Teacher's Guide*. www.theteachertoolkit.com/index.php/tool/turn-and-talk

Sumeracki, M. A., & Castillo, J. (2022). Covert and Overt Retrieval Practice in the Classroom. *Translational Issues in Psychological Science*, 8(2), 282–93. https://doi.org/10.1037/tps0000332

Sweller, J. (2006). The Worked Example Effect and Human Cognition. *Learning and Instruction*, 16(2 SPEC. ISS.), 165–9. https://doi.org/10.1016/j.learninstruc.2006.02.005

Sweller, J. (2021). Why Inquiry-Based Approaches Harm Students' Learning. *Analysis Paper (Centre for Independent Studies)*, 24 (August), 15.

Sweller, J., Ayres, P., & Kalyuga, S. (2011a). *Cognitive Load Theory*. Springer, New York. https://doi.org/10.1007/978-1-4419-8126-4

Sweller, J., Ayres, P., & Kalyuga, S. (2011b). The Guidance Fading Effect. In *Cognitive Load Theory* (pp. 171–82). Springer, New York. https://doi.org/10.1007/978-1-4419-8126-4

Sweller, J., & Sweller, S. (2006). Natural information processing systems. *Evolutionary Psychology*, 4, 434–58. doi:10.1177/147470490600400135

Thulasidas, M., & Gunawan, A. (2022). Cold Calls to Enhance Class Participation and Student Engagement. *2022 IEEE International Conference on Teaching, Assessment and Learning for Engineering (TALE)*, 699–702. https://doi.org/10.1109/TALE54877.2022.00122

Titsworth, S., Mazer, J. P., Goodboy, A. K., Bolkan, S., & Myers, S. A. (2015). Two Meta-Analyses Exploring the Relationship between Teacher Clarity and Student Learning. *Communication Education*, 64(4), 385–418. https://doi.org/10.1080/03634523.2015.1041998

Twyman, J. S., & Heward, W. L. (2018). How to Improve Student Learning in Every Classroom Now. *International Journal of Educational Research*, 87, 78–90. https://doi.org/10.1016/j.ijer.2016.05.007

Tyng, C. M., Amin, H. U., Saad, M. N. M., & Malik, A. S. (2017). The Influences of Emotion on Learning and Memory. *Frontiers in Psychology*, 8. https://doi.org/10.3389/fpsyg.2017.01454

van Harsel, M., Hoogerheide, V., Verkoeijen, P., & van Gog, T. (2021). Instructing Students on Effective Sequences of Examples and Problems: Does Self-Regulated Learning Improve from Knowing What Works and Why? *Journal of Computer Assisted Learning* (June), 1–21. https://doi.org/10.1111/jcal.12589

Vasilev, M. R., Kirkby, J. A., & Angele, B. (2018). Auditory Distraction During Reading: A Bayesian Meta-Analysis of a Continuing Controversy. *Perspectives on Psychological Science*, *13*(5), 567–97. https://doi.org/10.1177/1745691617747398

Wang, Y. (2022). To Be Expressive or Not: The Role of Teachers' Emotions in Students' Learning. *Frontiers in Psychology*, *12*, 737310. https://doi.org/10.3389/fpsyg.2021.737310

Ward, A. F., Duke, K., Gneezy, A., & Bos, M. W. (2017). Brain Drain: The Mere Presence of One's Own Smartphone Reduces Available Cognitive Capacity. *Journal of the Association for Consumer Research*, *2*(2), 140–54. https://doi.org/10.1086/691462

Wasik, B. A., & Hindman, A. H. (2018). Why Wait? The Importance of Wait Time in Developing Young Students' Language and Vocabulary Skills. *Reading Teacher*, *72*(3), 369–78. https://doi.org/10.1002/trtr.1730

Watkins, C. L., & Slocum, T. A. (2003). The Components of Direct Instruction. *Journal of Direct Instruction*, *3*, 4–32.

Willingham, D. T. (2021). Ask the Cognitive Scientist: Why Do Students Remember Everything That's on Television and Forget Everything I Say? *American Educator* (Summer). www.aft.org/ae/summer2021/willingham

Wong, M., Castro-Alonso, J. C., Ayres, P., & Paas, F. (2019). The Effects of Transient Information and Element Interactivity on Learning from Instructional Animations. *Advances in Cognitive Load Theory* (August), 80–8. https://doi.org/10.4324/9780429283895-7